YORK N

I0656775

COLD
MOUNTAIN

CHARLES FRAZIER

NOTES BY HELEN TREUTLER

 Longman

York Press

The right of Helen Treutler to be identified as Author
of this work has been asserted by her in accordance
with the Copyright, Designs and Patents Act 1988

YORK PRESS
322 Old Brompton Road, London SW5 9JH

PEARSON EDUCATION LIMITED
Edinburgh Gate, Harlow,
Essex CM20 2JE, United Kingdom
Associated companies, branches and representatives throughout the world

First published 2006

10 9 8 7 6 5 4 3 2 1

ISBN–10: 1–405–83567–2
ISBN–13: 978–1–405–83567–1

Illustrated by Neil Gower
Phototypeset by utimestwo, Northamptonshire
Printed in China

The author and publisher would like to thank Dr Fred J. Hay, Eury Appalachian Collection
Librarian at the Appalachian State University, for his help with glossing some of the lesser
known Appalachian dialect words and phrases.

CONTENTS

PART THREE
CRITICAL APPROACHES

PART FOUR
CRITICAL HISTORY

PART FIVE
BACKGROUND

PART ONE

INTRODUCTION

HOW TO STUDY A NOVEL

Studying a novel on your own requires self-discipline and a carefully thought-out work plan in order to be effective.

- You will need to read the novel more than once. Start by reading it quickly for pleasure, then read it slowly and thoroughly.

- On your second reading make detailed notes on the plot, characters and themes of the novel. Further readings will generate new ideas and help you to memorise the details of the story.

- Some of the characters will develop as the plot unfolds. How do your responses towards them change during the course of the novel?

- Think about how the novel is narrated. From whose point of view are events described?

- A novel may or may not present events chronologically: the time scheme may be a key to its structure and organisation.

- What part do the settings play in the novel?

- Are words, images or incidents repeated so as to give the work a pattern? Do such patterns help you to understand the novel's themes?

- Identify what styles of language are used in the novel.

- What is the effect of the novel's ending? Is the action completed and closed, or left incomplete and open?

- Does the novel present a moral and just world?

- Cite exact sources for all quotations, whether from the text itself or from critical commentaries. Wherever possible find your own examples from the novel to back up your opinions.

- Always express your ideas in your own words.

These York Notes offer an introduction to *Cold Mountain* and cannot substitute for close reading of the text and the study of secondary sources.

 **CHECK THE BOOK**

Michael McKeon's *Theory of the Novel: A Historical Approach* (2000) is an excellent introduction to the history of the novel.

READING _COLD MOUNTAIN_

CONTEXT

Walt Whitman (1819–92), generally considered to be one of America's finest poets, wrote his poetry without rhyme or formal rhythmic structure, which was considered experimental at the time. He published _Leaves of Grass_ in 1855, a work which celebrates individual freedom and the experience of common people. Whitman volunteered as a hospital nurse during the American Civil War and published _Drum Taps_, poetry about the war, in 1865.

CONTEXT

The Battle of Petersburg (15–18 June 1864) was followed by a long siege which lasted until March 1865. Union losses numbered 11,300; Confederate, 8,100. Neither side prevailed.

Charles Frazier's first novel was published to great acclaim in 1997. It seemed to recast the contemporary American novel into a new form, making use of several genres: romance, accounts of war, adventure, history and the natural world. An early review in the _New York Times_ (13 July 1997) spoke of a 'Whitmanesque foray into America: into its hugeness, its freshness, its scope and its soul' with 'a wealth of finely realised supporting characters'. The **epic** breadth of the story, the accounts of war in the landscape of North Carolina, will touch different chords in its readers.

The journey home from war is, for the central male protagonist, Inman, a spiritual quest for meaning as well as mere bodily survival. He faces a series of moral trials on his way through the American wilderness, much like Homer's Odysseus travelling home to Ithaca. He also has in him something of Christian in _The Pilgrim's Progress_, an **allegorical** moral work by John Bunyan from seventeenth-century Puritan England.

Setting interacts with character throughout the narrative: Inman must cross the 'sump of the continent' (Chapter 3, p. 65) to regain 'His place' (Chapter 15, p. 343). He travels through dangerous and inhospitable terrain to reach the North Carolina mountains, through valleys, forests, swamps and over a wide river, and each of the landscapes brings him personal challenges, internally and externally. A wealthy and affluent area even makes him question the imbalance of wealth and the people he is ostensibly fighting for. The journey home is the driving momentum and moves the whole narrative forward.

The American Civil War reverberates throughout the novel in catastrophic detail. Ordinary men are fighting, ordered by their generals who appear to have no pity or sense of perspective: at Fredericksburg 'they fall and keep falling until they are crushed' (Chapter 1, p. 9). At Petersburg the Federal tunnellers set off explosions: 'A column of dirt and men rose into the air and then fell all around' (Chapter 7, p. 153). And many non-combatant characters are traumatised by the war: maddened people who barely speak; the older woman whose entire family has died due to poverty and other knock-on effects of the conflict; Sara and her desperate clinging on to life without her husband, who was also killed in the war. The Federals and Home Guard seem to represent equal danger to the plain rural folk; most are living desperate subsistence and impoverished lives even before the war, and their suffering is redoubled by the conflict. Slavery and its remedies are touched upon; Inman is helped by outcasts in the gypsy camp and by a slave who feeds and shelters him. The human urge to give succour is presented by Frazier as tough and perennial.

A landscape which is suffering the disaster of war contains nonetheless an ideal spiritual dimension, represented by the mountain. Inman is isolated and traumatised by the war, and his task during his journey is to heal his inner psychic state so that he can re-emerge into some kind of relationship with people and the world. Cold Mountain itself, the ultimate physical goal of Inman's journey, represents for him wholeness and 'at oneness' with nature and himself. It is also 'home' in a human sense: it is the place where he will be reunited with Ada.

The mountain and the rhythms of nature are vast propelling forces in the novel and the seasons are instrumental in all that the characters do; even Ada, with her elevated outside culture, must put aside her novel to tend the fire. People's desires are played out against a capricious but ultimately nurturing universe; even Inman's death involves a 'bright dream of a home' with 'all the seasons blending together' (Chapter 20, p. 432).

We witness also the world of women who stay at home and wait, a tradition which has echoes in drama and prose from Greek tragedy to Shakespeare, from Jane Austen to Virginia Woolf, and in the contemporary diaries and letters of American Civil War wives. Female experience of war is recast for us: Ada's personal transformation and learning must refashion her into a woman worth the commitment of Inman. Ruby and her father represent Appalachian lore and proximity to nature, and bring humour to Ada's brooding abstract nature.

Frazier's style has been praised for its old world diction and **syntactical** structures; we approach his characters through the authentic language of the 1860s Appalachian people. Black Cove

CHECK THE BOOK

Virginia Woolf's *Mrs Dalloway* (1925) was for its time an experimental novel, employing the 'stream of consciousness' technique. The action of the novel shows a wealthy but somehow sidelined and separate woman reacting to her affluent post-war environment, and coming across a shell-shocked and suicidal man who forces her to alter her perceptions of herself.

CHECK THE BOOK

Cold Mountain has clear similarities with Homer's epic poem the *Odyssey*. Both stories show a hero returning after battle to his home and suffering much on the way. Penelope, Odysseus's wife, is the woman awaiting her husband's return.

and its nearby community speak and think in folkloric and rural terms; the counterpoint is Ada's rarefied Charleston upbringing, which she is prepared to substitute for the turning of the seasons and her new home.

Music, likewise, is a spiritual and levelling medium, speaking its own language; helping to heal and redress the balance towards peace and love in the final chapters. Myth and folklore across Western, Native American and Appalachian cultures give added resonance to all of the wanderings and changes felt by the characters.

Ultimately the novel is elegiac and unrelenting in its presentation of human suffering, and yet, in contrast, hopeful too. In spite of the waste and misunderstanding of civil strife, the future at the end is bright and even optimistic. The challenges the novel presents to the reader are around the relevance and fallout of war – how people are to survive a conflict which carries with it such far-reaching misery and retain meaning when moral chaos reigns. Finally it leaves us with questions about the value of home, of traditional values and our own emotional landscapes.

PART TWO

THE TEXT

NOTE ON THE TEXT

Cold Mountain was first published in 1997 by Grove/Atlantic, and won the National Book Award in the same year.

The text used for these Notes is that published by Sceptre Paperbacks, 1998.

SYNOPSIS

The novel contains two interwoven stories: one of Inman, a fugitive from the American Civil War, returning to his home in North Carolina; and the other of Ada, the woman he left behind when he went to war. In twenty chapters and an epilogue, the action swaps to and fro between the characters' respective lives. It opens with Inman in hospital with a severe wound in his neck; a conversation he has with a blind man about the Battle of Fredericksburg is depicted, followed by a trip into town, where he writes Ada a letter. He absconds from hospital and becomes an outlier, a fugitive from the war.

In a parallel narrative Ada is at home on Black Cove, a farm which she and her father moved to from Charleston several years before; she is struggling to live alone, after her father's death, as she is ill-equipped in temperament and knowledge. Her father, Monroe, was an idealistic man, who for the sake of his health moved to the mountains and took on a job preaching to a rural church congregation. He had brought her up in an atmosphere of educated sophistication. Her parents married late in life and Claire, her mother, died in childbirth.

Having heard of Ada's situation from local farmers the Swangers, Ruby, a stranger, appears at the farm and stays, helping Ada with the rough practical task of managing the land.

CONTEXT

The American Civil War began in April 1861, with the bombardment of Fort Sumter by the Confederates, and ended effectively on 9 April 1865 when the Confederate states surrendered to the Unionists at Appomattox Court House. Five days later, on 14 April, Abraham Lincoln was assassinated.

After travelling for some days, and in pain from his wound, Inman has to fight two men in a village, and then pays for help crossing the Cape Fear River. Inman remembers being introduced to Ada outside the church.

Ruby and Ada start work on the farm and Ada remembers the party held at her house, years before, when she and Inman embraced alone in the kitchen. Ruby's former life is explained – her early independence and the lack of a father who had gone to war are described.

Inman meets Veasey, a preacher whose lover is pregnant and whom he is about to murder. Inman prevents this, but begins to feel he is dodging the Home Guard. He stays at a camp of gypsies and outliers.

Ada and Ruby feed and give shelter for a night to a band of refugees from Tennessee. Ada remembers a party in Charleston before the war and a young recruit who wept in her presence, in fear of the war.

 CHECK THE NET
To help visualise Inman's journey, visit **www. worldatlas.com,** which has links to a range of North Carolina maps. There is also a map included in the **Background** section at the end of these Notes.

Inman and Veasey meet again and spend a night in a drover's inn, where Inman hears a story of disallowed love across the race divide from Odell, the estranged son of a rich farmer.

Ruby and Ada visit town and hear about Teague and his band of Home Guard rounding up and killing outliers. Ruby tells Ada that her mother had been raped by a heron to produce Ruby. Ada then recounts the story of her parents' marriage. They married late, and had brief happiness before her mother died in childbirth.

Inman and Veasey are tricked by a man, Junior, into returning to his farm, and are caught at his house by the Home Guard. Taken off with a band of prisoners, they are shot but Inman survives as the bullet passes through Veasey first. Inman returns injured to Junior's house to kill him. Later a slave on a farm helps him; he gives Inman food and shelter and a map to continue safely, as far as the mountains.

Ruby brings a letter from Inman to Ada. She remembers his departure when he told her the Shining Rocks **myth,** a Cherokee story about another legendary land like paradise. Their leave-taking was awkward and the next day Ada went to town to say goodbye again.

Next, Inman meets a goat woman who has lived alone for over twenty years in the mountains. She kindly gives him medicines, some of her philosophy on life and food to eat.

Ruby's father, Stobrod, turns up unexpectedly at Black Cove Farm, caught in a trap that Ruby had laid in the corncrib. He is living with outliers in a cave on the mountain. Stobrod eats with the women and plays music on his violin. Ruby grudgingly accepts his presence but refuses to take responsibility for him.

Inman stays at the cabin of a woman called Sara. Her husband has died in the war, she has a tiny baby, and she gives him food and clothes. When Federals attack her, Inman kills them and returns to her the hog they had stolen. He sleeps there for two nights, in her bed.

Stobrod brings a companion called Pangle to Black Cove and they play music for the women. Ada writes to Inman asking simply for him to return. Inman meets a woman with a dead child and helps her bury the girl. He sees three skeletons hanging in the woods and then encounters a mother bear and her cub. The bear charges him and falls over the cliff and Inman has to shoot the cub.

Stobrod, Pangle and a boy from Georgia search for the Shining Rocks on Cold Mountain. Teague and his Home Guard find the men and, after hearing their music and eating with them, shoot Pangle and Stobrod. The boy is apart from them in the woods and manages to escape to Black Cove to tell Ruby what has happened. The women set out to find the bodies.

They find Pangle, bury his body and find Stobrod alive. They stay in a deserted Cherokee village, which Ruby remembers from her childhood. Inman turns up at Black Cove expecting to see Ada and hears the story from the Georgian boy. Inman goes to find them. Ada shoots some wild turkeys and Inman hears the shots and finds her, dressed in men's clothes; he makes himself known to her. At first she does not recognise him; when she does so she leads him back to the village.

Inman now stays with the women and Stobrod through heavy snowfall. Ada and Inman are happy planning their future. The party decide to go back to Black Cove and separate to do so more safely.

CHECK THE FILM

Anthony Minghella's 2003 film *Cold Mountain*, shot in Romania, is a very successful version of Charles Frazier's novel; for students studying the novel, the rendition of atmosphere, dialect and culture of the Appalachian Mountains is particularly helpful.

Ada and Inman have decided he will cross the Blue Ridge Mountains to Virginia till the war is over and they can be reunited. But Teague and the Home Guard set upon Inman and Stobrod, in spite of killing all but one, Inman is himself shot and dies in the forest in Ada's arms. Stobrod escapes, saved by Inman.

The epilogue explains a time nine years later where the new family — consisting of Ada, Ruby, the Georgian boy and their three children, plus Stobrod and Ada's daughter, who was conceived in the Cherokee village — are eating a meal at the farm. Ada is in charge of her home, and the scene closes with a reference to the future: 'morning would dawn as early and demanding as always' and the safety the women have created in their new lives: 'Time to go inside and … pull in the latch string' (Epilogue, p. 436).

DETAILED SUMMARIES

CHAPTER 1: THE SHADOW OF A CROW

- We learn about Inman's current situation in hospital.
- We are given an account of the Battle of Fredericksburg.
- Inman prepares to leave hospital then absconds in the middle of the night.

The action opens in a military hospital where Inman, who has been gravely injured, is recuperating. In the next bed is a dying man, a scholar called Balis, who is learning Greek in his remaining days.

We learn that Inman survived via field hospital and train journeys and only very basic care in the current hospital. He walks outside to talk to a blind man who sells papers and peanuts; he tells him about the Battle of Fredericksburg where the Federal army sustained terrible losses, forced on by their own cavalry to certain death. Inman has witnessed huge numbers of deaths in the war, fighting on the Confederate side; and at Fredericksburg he was close to the Confederate generals, Lee and Longstreet, whose relish of fighting and killing he did not share.

Inman tells how that night the aurora appeared over a quiet battlefield and someone played 'the sad chords of Lorena' (p. 10). He has been left with nightmares since this battle.

Back on the ward, Inman reads a book called Bartram's *Travels*, which is an account of one man's wanderings in a range of mountains; it reminds Inman of his own home near Cold Mountain.

Soon after, he visits a nearby town and comes across a newspaper containing a warning to all deserters that they will be hounded by the Home Guard and killed. Another story of Cherokee killing Federals in the mountains takes Inman back to a youthful friendship with Swimmer, a sixteen-year-old Cherokee. Swimmer's close relationship to nature, his stories and spells are contrary to Inman's own upbringing and he gives Inman a racquet made of squirrel, bat and hickory wood to imbue him with their respective spirits.

Outside the inn, Inman writes a letter about the war, and in a second letter tells a loved one that the war has changed him. He posts this letter and returns to the hospital. Here he learns that Balis has died. He wakes in the middle of the night and absconds through the open window.

COMMENTARY

The action opens with a sense of recent trauma, physical and psychological, and a need to escape further wounding. War has inflicted extensive damage on Inman and a closely recounted memory of the Fredericksburg battle tells the reader about suffering and the chaos of war, as well as Inman's own part in the fighting. His recent recuperation has been patchy, and his body has rejected debris of the war, as if to reject its justification as well as its effects. He even wonders whether the debris will turn into something monstrous, possibly suggesting that Inman is feeling alienated from his own actions.

The present is harsh and unpleasant – 'the metal face of the age' (p. 2) stands in marked contrast to 'the old green places he recollected from home' (p. 2).

Through other vulnerable individuals, Balis and the blind man, we register some of the random savagery of war, suffering and pain.

CONTEXT

The Battle of Fredericksburg took place between 11 and 15 December 1862; Union casualties numbered around 13,000, largely due to the unsuccessful uphill attacks described by Inman, compared with Confederate losses of 4,500.

A longing to be returned to familiar surroundings fills this chapter; Inman seeks to re-engage with his former world and to find meaning in nature. There is a marked contrast between a relatively serene hospital setting and his haunting, nightmarish war memories. The narrative shifts back in time to his actions at Fredericksburg, and graphically delineates his contribution to the fighting: 'the slap of balls into meat' (p. 8). The closeness of enemy soldiers illustrates the arbitrary nature of wars fought between fellow human beings: 'one man jumped onto the wall and hollered out, You are all committing a mistake. You hear?' (p. 8).

CONTEXT

'The comeliest order …' is a quotation from the works of Heraclitus (544–483BC), a Greek philosopher whose view was that the cosmos was constantly in flux, and nothing stayed the same.

Inman is often described searching for meaning in this chapter, 'seeking the future in the arrangement of coffee grounds' (p. 19). He settles for the resignation he finds in Balis's notes: 'The comeliest order on earth is but a heap of random sweepings' (p. 22). This theme too will be revisited in the coming action as he encounters various versions of reality and seeks for a philosophy that encompasses all of human experience. His journey is therefore a mental and emotional one, with tests of his bodily endurance and moral fibre.

The battle scenes are recounted as recent events and they serve as rationale for Inman becoming a fugitive. He is strangely passionate and yet detached from his actions: 'Inman just got to hating them for their clodpated determination to die' (p. 9).

Other comfort comes from memories of Swimmer and his reading of Bartram's *Travels*. The Cherokee friend represents integration with nature: 'Swimmer would talk seamlessly in a low voice so that it merged with the sound of the water' (p. 17). Inman will later use Swimmer's spell when beset by depression and danger. Bartram has himself earned the name of Flower Gatherer from the Cherokee, for his habit of carrying plants in his satchels. Inman creates his own incantation, spurred on by Bartram's writing about mountains; the familiarity of the words has an effect on him rather like Swimmer's soothing voice and delivery. The presence of both Swimmer and Bartram's *Travels* suggests that Inman has resources to hand as he sets off for Cold Mountain.

GLOSSARY

2	**katydids** grasshoppers
	peepers frogs which make high-pitched sounds
3	**augured** drilled with holes
4	**boxcar** closed railway van
	flux diarrhoea
5	**peach pit** peach stone
6	**cinched** fastened at the waist
	razor strop piece of leather for sharpening a razor
	fraction a fight
7	**riddly spoon** spoon with holes
	drover someone who drives livestock to market
	hunker to sit on one's haunches
8	**unfletched arrow** arrow with no feathers
9	**clodpated** dull or stupid
10	**aurora** atmospheric phenomenon with bands of light in the night sky
	keened lamented and cried
	Potomac river in Virginia that rises in the Appalachian Mountains
14	**grits** coarsely ground wheat
15	**daguerreotype** early type of photograph
	balds bare mountain peaks
19	**wimple feathers** neck and head feathers
20	**éprouvette mortar** powder cannon

CONTEXT

The first hostilities of the American Civil War (12–13 April 1861) were at Fort Sumter in Charleston, a garrison sympathetic to the Federal cause. Fort Sumter came under bombardment from the Confederate forces on 12 April, and was forced to surrender the following day.

CHAPTER 2: THE GROUND BENEATH HER HANDS

- The reader learns about Ada's current life and recent history with her father.
- Ruby arrives at Black Cove and Ada agrees that she should stay.

The chapter summarises Ada's early life at Black Cove. As it opens she is writing a letter, but is dissatisfied with its tone. She is neglecting the farm and she rarely eats. To find eggs, she crawls into a bush and is attacked by a rooster.

CHECK THE NET

A fascinating website resource about the Home Guard can be found at **www.37nc.org**, giving information about 'rounding up conscripts and deserters' carried out by the 11th Battalion North Carolina Home Guard in the North Carolina mountains. It reminds us that all men aged forty-five to fifty and under the age of eighteen were 'required' to serve.

Ada's former life in Charleston is recounted; fine accomplishments, education, and acting as companion to her father, Monroe, are documented. She has been at Black Cove for six years and now loves Cold Mountain but initially felt like an outsider. In a flashback we learn how local people helped her deal with his death, and after the funeral Ada announced she would stay.

Ada picks up a letter at the post office and goes on to the Swangers' farm. The conversation there is of current events. As the state line is close by, there are stories of Federals crossing to loot farms, and Home Guard cruelty to local people. Ada reiterates that she will not return to Charleston. She agrees to use a local trick and looks backwards with a mirror down a well in order to see into the future. She sees a figure walking.

We hear how Monroe needed to move for his health and that he and Ada came to Cold Mountain in style. They arrived at a chapel late at night, having only guessed their route. In the morning they discovered it was their exact destination. Monroe's patronising style received mocking treatment from Esco Swanger. Although he had a house built at Black Cove, he did not run a productive farm, preferring to live on investments.

Back in the present narrative, the letter is from a solicitor saying that Monroe's investments are losing value. When Ada returns home she writes back saying she will take over her own financial affairs and will stay at Black Cove. Her decision is dictated by her wish not to marry under pressure or play the mating game.

At Black Cove, on the same evening, a woman arrives, having heard of Ada's situation from the Swangers. Her name is Ruby and they negotiate terms for her to work and live with Ada. She is confident in all the tasks of farm work. Ada finds out that, like her, Ruby has no mother. Ruby does not want to be paid but asks for equality in decisions and domestic tasks. Ruby kills the rooster and the women eat it for dinner.

COMMENTARY

Many conflicting elements in this chapter create a rich picture of farm life on the one hand, and cultivated values on the other, as well as social and gender issues, survival, food, friendship. We encounter isolation, hope and starting out again, what communities expect of their members and how individuals interact with their society.

As incomers, Ada and Monroe had been excited: Monroe quoted Wordsworth with a sense of elation as he arrived. However, the reality of life at Black Cove created conflict: Monroe believed he could tutor the community in Christian faith, via the intellect and Emerson; and Ada followed her father out of total reliance on his enthusiasm. The mockery they were subjected to showed that they had to work hard to adapt.

There are potential conflicts in this chapter between journeying and staying put, the sense of history and war close at hand versus the insularity of local custom. The issue of journeying to escape problems begins here, as do the issues of intellect versus reality and survival, history as a present force, and types of faith and belief.

The major mood of the chapter is of isolation; Ada is depicted as a woman out of her depth, groomed in city ways and customs. The relationship with her father had been central to her decision-making: 'I would follow this old man to Liberia if he asked me to do so' (p. 50). The counterpoint to this is her vulnerability now that he has died. Her major task now is to survive, and the narrative gains impetus from this, in her search for basics such as food, her fight with the rooster, her slightly desperate seeking out of company, and the fact that she is seen to have a better future once a stranger arrives.

Ada has internal conflicts: she turns down help from the solicitor, refuses to return to relatively safe prospects of marriage, but then conversely agrees to open her home to an entirely unknown person on the say-so of trusted local people.

The chapter makes use of flashback, or **analepsis**, to inform the reader of the recent past; this adds depth to our understanding of her decision. Ada is opinionated and vulnerable in close succession. We hear that she has wished for a 'fuller' life (p. 31) having read

> **CONTEXT**
>
> Indigo and cotton were the principal products of a healthy South Carolina economy, replacing rice in the late eighteenth and early nineteenth centuries. Monroe had investments in these crops.

narrow-mindedness

momentum

> **CONTEXT**
>
> Political issues around slavery, which formed a backbone to the success of the rural economy, led to South Carolina being the first state to secede from the Union in 1860; this in turn led to the bombardment of Fort Sumter in 1861 and eventually the American Civil War.

CHECK THE NET
For information regarding the books referred to and read by Ada, Monroe and Inman, visit **www.sc.edu/library**. Find the Rare Books and Special Collections page and follow the links to Charles Frazier and the Books of *Cold Mountain*.

The Mill on the Floss and *The Scarlet Letter*, both novels with female outcasts as central characters, yet we see her searching for eggs in a bush, and winding up at a neighbour's farm desperate to eat.

Local customs and tight communities are key to the narrative (those in Charleston as well as the mountains); accepting the beliefs of the rural community plays a significant part in the internal journey that Ada must make.

Ada's acceptance into the house of Ruby, a woman who appears as a half-**mythical** figure, barefoot and with toenails as 'pale and silver as fish scales' (p. 63), is indicative of Ada's need for sustenance and direction. Like her father, who had to deal with being mocked by the town for his abstract religious approach, Ada must find her place. There are already parallels in the characterisation of the two female characters with their common lack of a mother.

The well trick presages the final visit to Cold Mountain and Inman's reappearance in Ada's life.

GLOSSARY	
25	**poke** a tall North American plant with white flowers and juicy purple berries
	sumac small shrub with red hairy fruits
28	**secession** the withdrawal in 1860–1 of eleven Southern states from the Union
29	**treading** mating with (applies to birds)
	macassared oiled
30	**bookplate** owner's personal label in book
32	**palmettos** fan-shaped palms
	canted sloping or tilted
	the Edisto a river in South Carolina that flows to the Atlantic Ocean
33	**saleratus** bicarbonate of soda, used as a baking powder
	foxtails a species of grass
38	**croker sack** coarsely woven sack, previously worn by slaves
39	**withy** a willow used for weaving baskets
	cotter secure

41	**corncrib** a building used to store unhusked maize
48	**cabriolet** a small two-wheeled horse-drawn carriage
49	**wainwright** someone who makes wagons
50	**Liberia** an African country which began as a settlement for liberated black slaves from Southern states
53	**oracular** deemed to bring messages from oracles, foretelling the future
55	**dipped Baptists** belonging to the Baptist Church and baptised and initiated into that church
57	**boomer** squirrel
59	**woodlot** area restricted to growing of trees
	bobwhite a North American quail
	muntins bars across a window
61	**pomatum** hair oil
64	**gobs** lumps or chunks

CHAPTER 3: THE COLOR OF DESPAIR

- Inman continues his journey through a marsh, a small town, and across the Cape Fear River.
- The reader learns about the time Inman and Ada first met.

Inman's journey continues westwards towards Cold Mountain. He feels weak and downhearted; he is on unfamiliar territory. In a small town he buys provisions and is attacked by two men wielding a scythe; he fights back, and leaves the town. Inman remembers Swimmer's spell 'To Destroy Life' and uses it to protect himself (p. 72). This reminds him of Monroe's sermon and the first time he met Ada.

Inman recalls how he had heard of her arrival in town and sought her out by attending the church service. Monroe preached an intractable sermon, which puzzled the congregation. However, Inman appreciated it fully and engineered an introduction to Ada after the service. They had a stilted conversation that Ada brusquely concluded by walking away.

 CHECK THE FILM

Loosely based on Homer's *Odyssey, O Brother, Where Art Thou?*, directed by Joel Coen (2000), is set in Mississippi during the Great Depression. Three friends escape from a prison chain gang and set off on a search for love and fortune. Along the way they meet some strange characters, including a one-eyed man, sirens and a blind prophet.

Inman now comes to the Cape Fear River, in an ugly and inhospitable area, 'a sick and dangerous place' (p. 79). He finds a girl with a canoe who agrees to help him cross, for a high price. Chased by the men from the last town, they hide in the water, but escape as the river turns and carries them away.

COMMENTARY

The chapter contains present action with high levels of danger; in contrast is the peaceful past scene in which a potential romantic attachment began. In the current dangers Inman is seen to be proficient, even ruthless; meeting Ada he was out of his depth and gauche. Somewhat ill at ease in a wooing role, he is effective and dispassionate when fighting.

His walking is across dangerous emotional as well as physical terrain; he experiences the night as a set of hazards and attacks: 'every tree stump seemed to take on the shape of a lurker in the dark'; and he feels 'marked as the butt of the celestial realm, a night traveler, a fugitive, an outlier' (p. 67).

The narrative weaves together Inman's feelings and lessons learnt from Cherokee folklore alongside a high philosophical fragment of Ralph Waldo Emerson from Monroe's sermon.

A flashback details Monroe's abstract angle on life and sets up a rich counterpoint with the physical reality that besets Inman as an outlier. The chapter also indicates further depths by sketching some of his past character in the church scene. He half-heartedly belonged to a group of unsophisticated young bachelors, whose talk 'had more of Saturday night to it than Sunday morning' (p. 76). Inman's nature revealed something of the opportunist at this stage, and Ada's relative city sophistication disarmed and amused him. She was exotic: 'altogether foreign and beautiful and utterly awkward' (p. 76). His eventual approach was to parry her arch comments, and he hinted at future intimacy between them: 'Like grabbing up a chestnut burr, at least thus far' (p. 78). We see him bargain for an introduction to Ada with a promise to clear land, and ironically also later, for his passage across the river.

The description of Monroe suggests that he was intellectually zealous and aloof, unsuited to the new setting; Ada's ivory dress

---

CONTEXT

The philosopher Emerson (1803–82) was responsible for the emergence of **Transcendentalism**. He began life in a Unitarian family, and briefly became a Unitarian minister. Two of his important works are *Nature* (1836) and *The Conduct of Life* (1860), referred to later on in *Cold Mountain*. Monroe's attraction to Emerson placed him in a tradition of radical, intellectual religion that utilised philosophy for its major tenets, sometimes over the teachings of the Bible. Emerson himself became notorious for his proclamation that Jesus was a great man, but not God.

in winter showed she too was an outsider. In consequence the first conversation between Inman and Ada was abstract and on the level of language: each asked the other for an interpretation, and this theme of coding and understanding resurfaces throughout the narrative.

The landscape Inman walks through is unwelcoming, but 'It was, though, apparently the nature of the place' (p. 68). He can use a scythe, an implement from his former life, to cut down his enemies; he also has intimate knowledge of the workings of the Whitworth gun. The topography of the land he crosses takes the reader close to *The Pilgrim's Progress*, a classic work by John Bunyan focusing on the need for personal deliverance and cleansing in the face of sin: 'A miry slough indeed … the jangle of his own troubled mind' (p. 65).

Frazier uses rich figurative language to render Inman's state of mind; we see his personal antipathy as part of the landscape and its inclement nature. Depicted as 'God's most marauded bantling' (p. 65), Inman appears to wish for oblivion; this, on the other hand, adds to the narrative momentum to reach familiar terrain, 'getting home and building him a cabin on Cold Mountain', where, with Ada, 'there might be … hope' (p. 80).

Hope and despair meet head-on in this chapter. We are conscious of the effect war has on ordinary people: 'How did he ever think this to be his country and worth fighting for?' (p. 80). Inman's need for peace is especially emphasised – the 'right to exist unmolested somewhere' where 'not a soul but the nighthawks … could hear his sad cry' (p. 80). Ada also represents hope, if a rather chilly one. Tensions about survival and possible relationships are being developed in the narrative.

CHECK THE BOOK

For an interesting angle on the American Civil War, dip into E. L. Doctorow's *The March* (2005), which details the march led by Union General William Sherman through South Carolina in 1864, and the havoc wreaked by the Federal army as it travelled.

CONTEXT

The piedmont through which Inman travels had been resettled in the 1750s by Calvinist farmers who moved upcountry, and Anglican landowners who went on to establish the Anglican Church as the state church.

GLOSSARY

65	**bantling** a disparaging word for a young child
	pinebrakes areas of dense undergrowth and pine trees
	piedmont a low plateau between the Appalachian Mountains and flat land closer to the sea
	sullage sediment deposited by running water

continued

66	**clapboard farmhouses** characteristic farmhouses with overlapping wooden exteriors
67	**luna moth** a large pale green moth, with long wings
68	**loosed bedlamite** one who has been set free from a brutal mental asylum
	nipple pick cleaning pipe
69	**tarboosh** brimless cap often worn by Muslim men
	rounder an outspoken, blunt person
	tompion plug for muzzle of gun
71	**snath** handle of a scythe
73	**beardtongue** a flower with petals shaped like two lips
	jimson poisonous plant with funnel-shaped flowers
77	**pinchbeck** imitation gold
80	**scud** cloudy froth
82	**scrip** paper with a promise of money written on it
87	**a bed of duff** decayed leaves and branches

CHAPTER 4: VERBS, ALL OF THEM TIRING

- Ruby takes over the decision-making on Black Cove Farm.
- The piano is bartered for goods and provisions.
- Ada recalls a Christmas party at Black Cove where she ended up on Inman's lap.
- We are given an account of Ruby's early life, of poverty and survival.

CHECK THE FILM

The characterisation of Ruby in Anthony Minghella's 2003 film *Cold Mountain* makes use of comedy and pathos in equal measure.

Ruby is planning for the immediate future. As money has no real value now due to the war, Ruby's knowledge of how to rear animals, plant all manner of crops and how to barter and trade are critical skills for their future.

Ada agrees that she should let the piano be exchanged for goods. It is taken away and in return they receive livestock, corn, cabbages, ham and bacon. The piano reminds Ada of earlier Charleston days when her piano teacher fell in love with her and was dismissed.

The gig she wants to keep for the sense that she can always use it to ride away from her current life.

Ada remembers a time when her father put on a Christmas party for his neighbours. The account includes how Ada drank a lot of champagne and ended up sitting on Inman's lap in the kitchen. Some confused words passed between them. The rest of the party was uneventful, they talked briefly and he left.

Back in the present narrative, after the piano is gone, Ada finds a sack of coffee beans in the cellar, which is a great luxury. She and Ruby barter it for important goods.

Ada has lost an old habit of taking books everywhere on the farm. At evening time they rest, Ada reads from Homer and an account follows of Ruby's life.

She tells how her father and she lived in a shack with no real roof and little to eat. Ruby was forced to survive alone from a very early age. Her father, Stobrod, was an itinerant man who could commit to nothing beyond his own survival. Her account includes how, aged four, she spent an entire night caught on a thorn bush, terrified of the forest around her. Yet, later that night, nature seemed to give her assurance that she would live. She never shared this event with her father. When the war started her father enlisted, taking their horse, and was not heard of again. Ruby used the gun he left behind to hunt, and she made herself a knife.

Ruby knows the entire mountain, but she is not sure how old she is, as Stobrod had no recollection of her birth. She has no memory of her mother.

COMMENTARY

Ruby's character fills this chapter both in her resolved attitude towards the business of living, and the way in which the mystery of her life begins to unfold for Ada. She makes decisions which are instrumental in their survival, and helps also to clear out some of the impractical detritus of Ada's former life, symbolised in part by the piano. She teaches Ada to deal with reality: 'She held Ada's nose to the dirt to see its purpose' (p. 100). Her force as a principle of life is clear: 'Ruby would not let her fail' (p. 101). Her intimate

CHECK THE BOOK
Simon Schama's *Landscape and Memory* (1995) contains some illuminating discussion of cultural **myths**, touching on memory and experience of nature, as well as some references to American landscapes.

relationship to nature, symbolised by her night alone in the forest, explains to us the possible terrors of Cold Mountain. She undergoes a semi-rite of passage: 'she became like one born with a caul over one's face, knowing things others never would' (p. 103).

Ruby forces the pace, 'drawing up hard plans for the coming day that struck Ada as incongruent with its soft vagueness out the window' (p. 99). As in Charleston, Ada felt stifled at the party by the women's bawdy and earthy conversation about producing 'one baby after another' and 'dog hair in the gravy' (p. 95). A picture re-emerges of Ada being something of a humourless misfit.

The **flashback** of Monroe's party before the war has a quality of relative peace and order to it. There are sensuous descriptions, the tea 'fragrant with orange and cinnamon and clove' (p. 94), sentimental parlour tunes and champagne, all in marked contrast to Ada's current situation. The kitchen scene rekindles our interest in her odd self-conscious regard for Inman. There is intense sensuous imagery – 'the smell of his damp wool suit' (p. 97), 'the high lonesome baying of a grey wolf' (p. 96) – and a dizziness.

Much of the action at this point is remembered and memory acts as a rather shaky filter for the reader. However, small details act as a focus: 'a puzzled smile on his face and his hat lying crown down on the floor' (p. 97). There was a **foreshadowing** of the war at the end of the evening when the men left 'firing their pistols toward the heavens' (p. 98).

Ruby's former life is told as a series of lacks – of roof tiles, floor, clothes, food and fatherly love. Stobrod is characterised as a feckless irresponsible man, but she had instead the 'tender force of landscape or sky' to protect her (p. 103). His past misdeeds nonetheless caused her pain, but as with Ada, whose mother was also absent during her childhood, a factual and detached tone presents to the reader the rudiments of survival: 'She guessed that Stobrod had not warred for long' (p. 105).

Stobrod's vagueness about when Ruby was born is reminiscent of her first arrival at Black Cove, where she seems to evanesce into

 CHECK THE NET
An interview with Charles Frazier about *Cold Mountain* can be found at **www.reading groupguides.com** – search for Charles Frazier; there is also an interesting small section of critical quotations on the novel.

view as a force of nature. Ada's world, in contrast, is recounted as a series of fully tangible phenomena, from sitting on Inman's lap, to feeling her nose was too big, to chopping off the head of a chicken and seeing her hands as 'the claws of a beast' (p. 100).

> **? QUESTION**
>
> What is Ruby's angle on life and how does she balance Ada?

GLOSSARY

88	*maul* heavy hammer
	froe a cleaving tool
89	*boluses* food for horses to chew
	spurge plant with milky juice
	yarrow plant with healing properties
	guineas dark feathered, plump farm birds
90	sorghum water water with syrup added
91	dapple gelding male horse with mottled coat
92	naphtha aromatic chemical made from petroleum
93	shoat piglet
94	bead froth
96	qualmish nauseous
99	roust stir
100	shakes roof tiles
101	sot drunkard
	scofflaw criminal or debtor
	tick mattress cover
102	hants ghosts
103	caul amniotic sac covering a newborn baby's head
104	mast pig food made from forest tree fruits
	tow sack coarse-fibred sack
105	hinny mule
	minié French rifle
	harquebus portable gun from the fifteenth century

CHAPTER 5: LIKE ANY OTHER THING, A GIFT

- Inman saves Laura from being murdered by her lover.
- He comes across a camp of show folk and gypsies with whom he eats and spends one night.
- They disappear the next morning.
- Inman dreams of Ada.

Inman walks at night along the Deep River and sees a man leading a horse with a white load slung over its back, which, Inman discovers, is an unconscious woman. The man is crying and explains to Inman that he is a preacher and the woman, Laura, is his pregnant lover.

Inman commands the man to take all three of them back to their home town. Unsure of what to do for the best, as they travel Inman sees the Orion constellation in the sky and is reminded of a soldier who, after the Fredericksburg battle, asserted that the human urge for knowledge was pointless. Inman decides they will take the woman back to her home, but he ties the preacher to a tree before they arrive. Taking Laura into her house, past her sleeping grandmother, Inman tells her when she stirs not to trust the preacher. She falls asleep again. Inman writes the account of the preacher's actions on paper, and pins it above his head on the tree.

We hear Inman is skilled in fighting with unclouded judgement. He passes two slaves driving a hog and then follows the smell of cooking food. He sees a camp of outliers and gypsies and enters the camp with hands out in a gesture of surrender. Inman is fed and is safe for a day at the camp.

Inman watches a young woman mounting and riding a horse. He hears a conversation in which a man suggests that one day the word 'slave' may be only a turn of phrase and not literal. Inman settles to sleep near the camp and reads Bartram's *Travels* to calm his mind. The sight of the show woman and the feel of Laura earlier as he carried her take him back to the kitchen memory with Ada sitting on his lap. He remembers holding her hand and kissing her wrist.

CONTEXT

William Bartram's *Travels*, published in 1791, is used by Inman to lift his spirits as he walks, and builds further geographical reference points for the modern reader. Frazier has characterised Bartram as 'one of the great nature writers'.

He falls asleep and dreams of a forest with Ada as a vague figure. He tells her he will stay with her for ever and wakes to find the camp deserted.

COMMENTARY

This is a chapter of opposites – the sordid and pathetic story of the preacher and the girl he comes close to murdering, and Inman's meting out of justice; and the brief comfort and safety of the camp of social outcasts, with their non-establishment values.

We learn of Inman's cynicism and hard-won realism early on in the phrase 'the rare goodwill of the random world' (p. 115), and also his recognition that human influence is at best trivial and at worst pernicious. He is especially cutting about the preacher's actions: 'you with your britches around your ankles' (p. 113). He even feels the natural order is damaged, like a 'wound in the earth' (p. 107).

On the other hand we see his tender treatment of Laura: 'Inman … touched her brow and brushed back the hair where it curled at the temples' (p. 116). Inman redresses the moral balance: 'He means you no good. Set your mind on it' (p. 116). But we witness also his vulnerability: coming across slaves he is at his lowest so far and 'wished … he were a big red hog and could just lie down and wallow' (pp. 119–20).

The encounter with the camp people creates contact with permanent outsiders, and they offer a new sense of order, for they are 'as outlaw and Ishmaelite as himself' (p. 120). The war itself fades into perspective in this chapter as a backdrop and 'no more to them than a temporary hindrance to business' (p. 121).

In an echo of Ada's well trick, Inman declines having his fortune told. He is more defensive, as 'he figured he already had all the discouragement he needed' (p. 121).

The description of Laura is sensual, as is that of the gypsy woman as 'she caught up the hems of her long skirt and petticoat' (p. 122); these details remind us of the physical reality of Inman, and they have echoes in his dream of Ada, who starts off as a dreamlike

? QUESTION

There are many dispossessed groups in the novel, from gypsies and women, to poor farmers, manipulated soldiers, African Americans and Native Americans. How does Frazier use his novel to explore the ways certain groups have power over others?

vision before becoming flesh and blood. The memory of her at Monroe's party as she sat on his lap is conveyed with immediacy: 'The softness of her, and yet the hard angularity of her bones underneath' (p. 125).

A social factor is at play also for Inman as the people, 'all of a color and equals', scour their own plates after their meal (p. 123). Context is added with the suggestion that slavery may be at an end one day. The ephemeral nature of the camp contrasts with the immediacy of the people and their activities. As with the memory of Ada, they were once real and are now faded.

Inman has a number of faces in the chapter: an avenger and saviour for Laura; then a fellow outcast from society; and lastly, in his memory and dream, a man of emotion and commitment: 'I'm never letting you go. Never' (p. 127).

CONTEXT

In the Bible Ishmael was the son of Abraham and Hagar, the handmaid of Abraham's wife Sarah; Hagar and Ishmael were driven into the wilderness by Sarah after the birth of her child Isaac (Genesis 21).

GLOSSARY

107	swale low marshy land
108	sconce bracket for a candle or torch
109	bluff steep river bank
115	batten boards a traditional building technique for North Carolina wooden homes
	stoop a step
118	hexes curses or spells
	ingot shaped piece of metal
120	Ishmaelite an outcast (from the Old Testament; compare Joseph's years as an outcast from his family, living with the Ishmaelites, Genesis 37:18–36)
	spavins and bots and heaves all horse diseases, of legs and bowels
123	cachexia weight loss
125	petioles plant stalks
	panicles clusters of flowers

CHAPTER 6: ASHES OF ROSES

- At Black Cove a band of refugees are fed and given shelter for a night.
- Ada tells Ruby about a party at Charleston.
- Ada feels contentment at Black Cove.

CONTEXT

'The law requires that each County of the State shall contribute its proportion of men for the war, and those counties deficient will be drafted until its quota is made up.' These words are taken from a speech made by a Confederate general in North Carolina in February 1862, from an essay entitled 'Civil War in the Mountain South'.

Ruby and Ada are hard at work ploughing and planting food for the winter. Ruby follows nature for its signs as she decides which tasks to tackle first. Ada respects Ruby's sensitivity to the natural order.

On this afternoon, a band of women and children refugees pass the farm, lost, and heading for South Carolina. Ada and Ruby discover that they are victims of the Federals and have been burnt out of their homes, as well as robbed. The women cook for their visitors. Next morning the travellers have breakfast, Ruby gives them a map for their journey and they leave.

Ada and Ruby have lunch down in the orchard and Ruby tests Ada on her knowledge of nature and practical matters. Ruby has learnt about nature from a variety of females in her childhood. She explains how all the phenomena of the seasons are connected. Ruby then sleeps in the orchard and Ada walks off observing flowers and birds and the general movement of insects; she experiences a sense of contentment.

That evening Ada reads to Ruby from Homer. Ruby's take on the Odysseus story is suspicion for a man who takes such a long time to get home after the war.

A memory of a Charleston party surfaces for Ada and she tells it to Ruby. It was a three-day affair, sophisticated and lavish, at a mansion belonging to Ada's cousin Lucy. Monroe bought a whole bolt of cloth for Ada so that no one else would have a similar dress. The party had an extra edge due to the war fever felt by the men as they left to fight. Ada tells how she reluctantly agreed to go on the river with a man named Blount. He was determined to join up and asserted he would defend the values of the Confederacy. Ada did not respond with the expected patriotic phrases and he quietened. She then remembers how he told of his fears of the fighting, and of the terrible death he expected to be his fate. He wept and Ada showed sympathy by stroking his hand but said nothing. He composed himself and rowed the boat back to the bank. She recalls he gave her a brotherly kiss as they parted.

Ada recounts that back inside the mansion, she caught sight of a woman in a mirror, looking self-assured and in control, and then realised it was herself. The next day Blount was embarrassed as the party broke up, and would not look at Ada; Ada heard later of Blount's death at Gettysburg, where, ordered to retreat, he walked backwards and was shot in the face.

Ruby's response to this story is cursory and unsympathetic. Ada remembers Monroe and how he felt Black Cove and the mountain were representative of another world. Now, in this moment, Ada feels that Black Cove encompasses the whole of life. When she steps into the patch of field the cow had vacated she works her fingers into the warm earth and grasps handfuls of the soil.

COMMENTARY

The chapter further details Ruby's husbandry of her immediate world and shows her communion with nature: 'everything ... fell under the rule of the heavens' (p. 129). Another stage in Ada's acceptance of this natural lore is described; she re-encodes Ruby's values as 'an expression of stewardship, a means of taking care, a discipline' (p. 129).

Ada is contented in her new life with Ruby. The world of Black Cove seems to contract around the women and the daily and seasonal order establishes the rhythm of their lives. Ruby's voice is heard in her dialect: 'November, we'll kill a hog in the growing of the moon' (p. 129).

The lost victims of Tennessee remind us of the scale of destruction caused by war. Ruby and Ada are relatively rich in resources as they are able to offer food and shelter to the visitors. They hear also of the stripping of the women's goods: 'every bit of food we had been able to raise this year' (p. 130), which has some **ironic** force in that this determination to provide for themselves matches that of Ruby and Ada. The female angle on war receives treatment here.

Via the account of the Tennessee women, Ada, Ruby and the reader discover that the Federals are hostile to women and children too, and the common job of survival briefly expands the insular world of Black Cove. Yet they are reminded of their good fortune: 'You are luckier than you know, hid in this cove' (p. 131).

We learn how Ruby has gathered her skills 'from wandering around the settlement talking to any old woman who would talk back' (p. 132). This further contributes to the picture of female stamina and kinship emerging from this chapter.

Ada's memory of the party is described in **lyrical** and ethereal terms; it clearly belongs to a distant past. Her memories are sharply delineated for the reader and we recognise the **dissonance** between a wealthy Ada who had a dress made out of a whole bolt of material, and her current straitened circumstances. Ruby also has a sharp cynical response to Ada's account of the party, and marvels at 'lives so useless that they required missing sleep and paddling about' (p. 138). Their previous lives have had little in common.

Ada has a new comfortable relationship with the physical world. The past is relegated: 'The colours that had reminded her of Charleston were now muted. Everything declining toward stillness' (p. 139). Monroe's version of Black Cove, as a metaphor, is now invalid for Ada; touching the ground beneath the cow's haunches, she feels that it is as 'warm as a living thing' (p. 140). Charleston is replaced in Ada's world by palpable and closely observed realities, with Ruby as 'her principal text' (p. 132).

See **Text 1** of **Extended commentaries** for further discussion of part of this chapter.

CHECK THE FILM

Anthony Minghella's 2003 film *Cold Mountain* shows a warm and companionable relationship between Ada and Monroe; to what extent do you feel this is reflected in the book?

GLOSSARY	
128	joe-pye weed weed with purple-coloured flowers
133	sumac red hairy-fruited plant
134	ironweed purple-flowered shrub
	dog hobble evergreen shrub *continued*

CONTEXT

In the 1860s huge cattle ranches had been established in Texas and settlement was increasing rapidly. Veasey has heard of the riches to be had – 'a piece of land the size of a county' (p. 146) – and wishes to join the push out to the ranches in order to begin a new life. Texas, the twenty-eighth state to join the Union in 1845, was the seventh to secede from it on 1 February 1861.

CONTEXT

Churching was a rite carried out on women after childbirth or if they had committed incest, fornication or adultery. The rite could include being blessed, praise being offered for the birth of a child, or being disallowed from attending church as a punishment.

| 135 | bolt of cloth a roll of cloth for dressmaking |
| 137 | Argand lamps gas-burning lamps |

CHAPTER 7: EXILE AND BRUTE WANDERING

- Inman steals food from women washing clothes in the river.
- The preacher, Veasey, reappears.
- Veasey attempts to rob a store, and Inman intervenes.
- They stop at a drovers' inn.
- Inman hears Odell's story of love for a slave.

The chapter opens with Inman meeting a range of slightly maddened people, then a trio of girls dancing in the dust, and women washing clothes by a river. He steals food and hides from another walker who turns out to be Veasey, the preacher Inman had tied to the tree. Veasey tells of the punishment he received from his town, and describes what he imagines will happen to the woman, Laura, once it becomes apparent that she is pregnant: 'she will be churched for a time' (p. 145). He now wants to travel to Texas and make his fortune.

Inman takes some honey from a gum tree. He and Veasey chase a catfish and kill it. Veasey questions Inman about his origins but Inman remains silent. Inman tells a story about a battle at Petersburg where tunnellers from the Federal side blew through to behind the Confederate line, and were butchered in the crater they had created.

Next day the men come to a store; Veasey attempts to rob the storekeeper, but Inman intervenes. They eventually reach a drovers' hostel on the roadside. Inman again stops a fight between Veasey and another man. A huge woman, Tildy, serving drinks, offers sex to Veasey for money.

Inman pays for a bed in the hayloft and comes across a peddler, Odell. They drink together and Odell's story is told in some detail. He tells how he had an affluent life as the son of a plantation owner in Georgia, and was married to another plantation owner's daughter.

He subsequently fell for a slave called Lucinda who had been won by Odell's father at gambling. Odell told his father he loved her and his father instructed him to take her by force to satisfy his desire. The next day she was rented to another family. Odell had an affair with her and when Lucinda told him she was pregnant, Odell asked to buy Lucinda from his father. He was locked up on the plantation and Lucinda disappeared.

The story continues with Odell stealing money from his father's safe and leading the life of a peddler, travelling around with only a barrow, and expecting to slide further down the social ladder in the future. His story includes accounts of lynching of black slaves, and a woman locked in a cage, left to be eaten by buzzards.

The next morning, Inman leaves the inn and Veasey follows after him, with a razor cut on his face as recompense for disagreeing over Tildy's price.

COMMENTARY

The chapter has at its heart a heavy contrast between the searing tragedy of the disallowed interracial love of Odell and Lucinda, and the reckless, inappropriate stupidity of Veasey, the erstwhile preacher. Inman acts as a sounding board to both men as they tell of their experiences, offering in particular a quiet understated 'It's a feverish world' (p. 167) to the dreadful suffering of the slaves in Odell's story. But to Veasey he is denigrating and ambivalent.

The trauma of war is again present in his story of Petersburg: 'war in its most antique form' (p. 153), which is followed by a cutting question to Veasey: 'There's the sort of thing you missed … You sorry?' (p. 154).

A contradiction is opening up again for the reader in Inman's apparent patience with Veasey, who is more of a burden than a companion. The fact that Inman saves him twice from violence, kills the fish and collects the honey for him is contradictory to his spoken criticisms of Veasey. Veasey's character adds some lightness to the account, even if only in terms of his wavering, pragmatic code: 'God will not strike you too hard for leaning in the direction of your hungers' (p. 149). Veasey shows other depths too with his

> **? QUESTION**
>
> Veasey quotes the Bible at will and utilises its sententious style to make strong assertions. What significance does Veasey's selective interpretation of scripture have for his character and the theme of religion in *Cold Mountain*?

story of Legion 'fleeing mankind, hiding in the wilderness' (p. 152), which acts as a comment on Inman's own state.

The story of plantation life is contextually important for the reader, expressing as it does a harsh picture of the South: men and women being sold and caged, a father meting out punishment to his son, indulgences of gambling, drinking and great wealth. The central issues are land which is 'too much to bother measuring in acres' (p. 162), and love which is 'a mark of an unsound mind'. More basically, the chapter deals also with Veasey buying sexual favours from 'Big Tildy', and their encounter ends in a razor cut when she gets the better of him.

Inman witnessed idealism and comfort at the gypsy camp, and now survival is again a practical and hard-nosed affair. Contrasting paternal relationships are displayed; in a rare mention of Inman's own father, we hear how he learnt to collect honey from bees' nests.

The women in the chapter are either idealised: 'the fine bones of her hands and feet and ankles' (p. 163); or baldly described as suffering agony: 'the woman vomited blood and died' (p. 167) and in sexual terms, as with Big Tildy, and Odell's wife: 'little there to keep his mind from wandering' (p. 163). The women washing in the river are likened to a regiment of Zouave soldiers with their bright pantaloons; in a sensual moment Inman sees the water running off legs that 'glistened in the light like oil' (p. 143), but decides to focus instead on their food and not their bodies.

CONTEXT

The Zouave soldiers fashioned themselves on North African troops in the French Army; they were flamboyantly dressed in coloured pantaloons, and fought with dash and vigour on both sides of the conflict.

GLOSSARY

141	pikes medieval weapons
	persimmons an orange-red fruit
144	mendicant friar a begging monk who has taken an oath of poverty
147	pistolero Spanish gunman
	mullein and burdock brightly coloured plants
149	galax white-flowered perennial
151	ballpeen hammer round-headed hammer
153	wattled trenches trenches with fences lining the sides
	parching rye roasting some rye grains

Ada's parents; and a fearful picture of how the Home Guard round up and punish outliers. We meet the character of Teague for the first time, and recognise the threat that he presents to Inman as he attempts to get home to Cold Mountain. A sense of pernicious and angry fate is present in the chapter: 'a dark-fisted hand seemed poised ready to strike at any moment' (p. 184).

The two women share their sense of their roots; Ruby's brief story of the heron is the improbable stuff of legend, contrasting in length and human detail with Ada's parents' frustrated but finally fruitful relationship.

The heron section of the chapter works with metaphors of isolation, exile and the hermit life: Ada sees them as 'so lonesome as to make the heart sting on their behalf'. Looking at the heron, Ada tells Ruby of a Greek myth of vanity and Ruby responds with: 'Stab wounds; that's his main nature' (p. 185). Likewise, Ada is cut down to size by Mrs McKennet when she offers her view that the war is 'Degrading to all' (p. 174).

Teague clearly presents a fearful risk for any outlier, and his victims appear hopelessly vulnerable in their weaponry and naive in their art of fighting; Teague in contrast is casual and heartless: 'Come on out, Teague called. There was a note of the festive to his voice' (p. 180).

The story of Ada's parents is narrated in the language of wooing and total commitment. Monroe told his daughter: 'I have never seen the match to her. There is not a word for how beautiful she looked to me' (p. 189). In contrast, Ruby's mother's experiences are harsh and humiliating: 'a flogging of dreadful scope' (p. 187).

On their walk, myth and reality intertwine again as Ruby and Ada see a woman carrying a baby and skipping barefoot 'as graceful as a deer', and witness nature's repetitive codes: 'The thing their pattern of flying told was more rain' (p. 187). After the harrowing suffering of the last two chapters, the final quiet moment of this chapter – 'The blue one, that brighter one, is Venus, Ada said' (p. 194) – resettles the narrative in favour of nature and its comforting patterns.

CONTEXT

In Greek mythology Narcissus, the most handsome of young men, fell in love with himself, gazing at his reflection in a pool, and died of sorrow.

GLOSSARY

168	**poplin** clothing fabric
	toting a rifle looking like a huntsman carrying a rifle
169	**spurge** milky-juiced plant
170	**a plug of chaw** a piece of chewing tobacco
174	**peck basket** a basket to carry eight quarts
175	**sordor** sordidness
176	**malandered about the necks** with froth on their necks
184	**jouncing** roughly jolting
185	**anchorite** someone living a secluded religious life
186	**picket** lookout or sentinel watching for something to happen
189	**cow-hocked** with ankle joints like a cow
	palmettos palm trees
190	**tow sacks** sacks made of coarse fibre
191	**yaupon** holly with yellow berries

 QUESTION

The local language or **vernacular**, which Frazier uses for many of his characters, has been recognised by some commentators as a distancing device in *Cold Mountain*. How much do you agree that the dialect separates the characters from modern readers' experiences?

CHAPTER 9: TO LIVE LIKE A GAMECOCK

- Inman and Veasey meet Junior and help him shift a dead ox.
- They walk with Junior to his house and meet his family.
- Inman and Veasey are arrested by the Home Guard, and Inman is tricked into 'marriage' with one of the women.
- The prisoners are taken by the Home Guard and shot in the woods; Veasey dies and Inman survives.
- A slave gives him food and shelter.
- Inman returns to Junior's house and kills him.

Inman and Veasey find a saw, which Veasey intends to steal. Inman questions Veasey on his dubious morality and Veasey's views are that justice is random. They see a man who tells how his water is blocked off and asks for help with moving a carcass of a bull from a creek. He offers them food and shelter for the night. They all drink together and the man, named Junior, tells of his days fighting cocks for money, and also of his sexual adventures.

At Junior's house, a dilapidated, sloping shack, it having shifted on its foundations, they have more to drink and meet Junior's wife, her sisters and various children of the family. The women are graphically and sexually described and Junior treats them abusively.

Veasey falls asleep. The children say nothing and move around in odd formation. They are given strangely shaped bread to eat. Lila tells Inman of a time when Junior killed a man and a dog and put the heads on a tree stump. Inman hides his bag, beginning to feel disorientated and drunk. Lila sends the others away, and sits herself on the table in front of him offering sex.

Junior suddenly appears with a gun, and tells Inman: 'What you about to learn is they ain't no balm in Gilead' (p. 212). Inman prepares to die. The Home Guard also appear and Inman and Veasey are tied up. A mock wedding takes place with Inman and Lila as bride and groom, and the Home Guard then take Inman and Veasey away, along with their other prisoners.

The prisoners are marched through the forest for days and Inman feels he is going back over his old tracks. The men are distressed, rarely eat and can only sleep in a pile to keep warm. One night the Guard order them to stand up and they raise their guns to kill them. Inman again prepares to die. The shot that hits him passes through Veasey first and he falls. The guards bury the men in a shallow grave, and Inman lies there all night. The next morning, he is roused by hogs digging him out.

After tending his wound, Inman is helped by a slave and given food and shelter at a farm for a few days. The slave gives him a detailed map of the journey west and warns him of the patrols out looking for Federals who have broken out of jail. Inman is surprised that the slave can read and write, and is told the slave's master ignores the law. With no money to give the slave, Inman leaves.

Some days later he arrives at Junior's house and kills him. He carries on walking and takes care to melt into the landscape.

COMMENTARY

The action in this chapter is fast paced and cumulative. Beginning with the saw and ox incident and ending with the revenge on Junior,

CHECK THE BOOK

The three sisters at Junior's house have connections to the sirens in the *Odyssey*, female temptation figures who lure men to certain destruction.

CONTEXT

The reference to Gilead is from Jeremiah 8:22 in the Old Testament, where the prophet asks: 'Is there no balm in Gilead?' Junior reverses the meaning and uses the phrase metaphorically to suggest that Inman is about to suffer.

Inman is beset by chaotic behaviour which evades comprehension: 'The world moved on about him and he observed it, though he felt not a part of it. It seemed to scorn understanding' (p. 219). He is one of the caught fugitives who are 'bearing the burden of lives lived beyond recollection' (p. 217). A reference to a higher level of existence fashions some perspective: 'the stars had drawn together in congress and agreed to flee, to shed light on some more cordial world' (p. 213).

Veasey's reckless behaviour is a risk to them both. Junior's deceit is seen against the backdrop of his extreme poverty, both financial and spiritual. But the callous treatment of his entire family offers as bleak a picture of human nature as the novel has given so far. The children are traumatised and shuffle rather than play. References to devils and spectres are frequent, so that the sloping house seems devoted to half-deranged behaviour.

The mock wedding has a grotesque mysticism attached to it, and the song that Junior sings in the ceremony, 'modal and dark' (p. 215), refers to the desperate times in which they live. Even Inman, so hardened by the degree of death he has witnessed that 'it seemed no longer dark and mysterious' (p. 221), feels compelled to testify to the callous behaviour of the Guard: 'I do not understand you people' (p. 216).

Veasey is given a strangely evangelical line: 'It is not too late to put away this meanness' (p. 219), which ironically reminds us of his earlier moral statements. However, his death suggests that it may indeed be too late for moral chaos to be averted.

Sympathy for the common man emerges as a theme. Most of the prisoners are 'country people in homespun' who would 'pass from the earth without hardly making any mark more lasting than plowing a furrow' (p. 216). Veasey's vain ambitions are thrown into sharp relief against the random and enormous suffering of these ordinary people.

Some alleviation of suffering is presented with the slave who takes Inman in and feeds him. Although the action of the chapter is apparently hopeless, Inman retains his own idealistic thoughts of becoming a crow so 'he still had power either to fly from enemies or laugh them away' (p. 226).

CONTEXT

Through Junior's grotesque mimicking of a marriage ceremony, a picture emerges of a man who twists spiritual values and rites.

CONTEXT

In this part of North Carolina, Moravians and Quakers lived in the region near the foothills of the Blue Ridge, as shown in the map from the slave who helps Inman. They had settled there having left persecution behind in Europe, and formed a community of small farms with free rather than slave labour.

GLOSSARY

197	sisal rope fibre made from a plant
200	dominicker a breed of hardy cockerel which can forage well
202	treed and shot trapped and shot
204	cathouse brothel
205	towheaded white or blonde
207	scut tail or backside
	hantlike like ghosts
208	homunculus miniature human-shaped form
210	canted tilted
	lucent shining
	nary no
211	behexed bewitched
214	stoups drinking cups
	jenny barn a brothel
	buck-and-wing boisterous tap dance
	getting into the shortrows having sex
215	prothalamion song to celebrate marriage
216	harns brains
217	spoor tracks
218	Psalter book of psalms
223	chines of pork pig's backbone

CHAPTER 10: IN PLACE OF THE TRUTH

- Ruby and Ada set a trap in their corncrib.
- Ada makes a scarecrow out of her mauve party dress.
- Ada receives a letter and remembers Inman's departure four years before.

Ruby and Ada mend fences and set a trap to deter a corn thief. Ada makes a scarecrow, using her old dress from the last party at Charleston. When Ruby arrives back with more provisions than

WWW. CHECK THE NET

Salisbury was the fifth largest city in North Carolina by 1860. The Salisbury Prison website – **http://salisbury prison.gorowan. com** – provides a wealth of information, photos and some first-hand accounts of the Confederate prison in Salisbury, where over 11,000 Union soldiers are said to be buried.

expected, she hands Ada a stained letter she has been given at the mill. Ada wants to read it alone.

The women dig some trenches behind the smokehouse to store some cabbages for winter use. Later on they braid each other's hair. We hear something of Ruby's attitude to travel and the outside world, which Ada does not contradict. The women look at the results of the braiding and Ruby insists Ada has won; she does the night-time chores as Ada's prize. Ada has read Inman's letter, which shows commitment towards her. She speculates on when the letter was written, and what it means. Her memory of the Teague story frightens her. In the letter Inman has told her not to look at a photograph he gave her as he has changed hugely; Ada goes to look at it in her bedroom. We hear how Monroe, when he saw it, quoted from Emerson about the falseness of the human image in photographs.

A **flashback** recounts a memory of Inman's goodbye before he went to war. He came to see Ada, she recalls, and they went down to the river for a walk. Ada remembers how she didn't voice her fears about the war and barely said anything to comfort Inman. He then told her a story of Shining Rocks, a legend in which another, happier, world appeared in the mountain and was then taken away. This legend was told to him by an old woman who had hidden when the army came to round up the Cherokee before forcing them on the Trail of Tears. Ada was unsentimental and terse in response and they parted with few words. Later on Ada was uncomfortable about Inman's departure and wished she had been less cool towards him. She passed an uncomfortable night, feeling deep physical longing for him. Her cousin Lucy had told her that physical and sexual pleasure was not an immoral thing, even when one gave oneself that pleasure. Unused to the male body, she fell asleep fantasising about Inman's hands and arms.

Her memory continues with her taking the coach next day into town with Monroe. She looked for Inman and tried to tell him she wished she had said other warmer things to him. She recalls now that they kissed and parted, both expressing a wish to see each other soon.

CONTEXT

The Trail of Tears from 1838 to 1839 is a much-lamented period of persecution in the history of the Cherokee. The Native Americans were forcibly ejected from their land, following the Indian Removal Act of 1830, and compelled to make a thousand-mile journey on foot to a reservation in Oklahoma. Four thousand people died on the trail.

COMMENTARY

The chapter focuses on the relationship between Ada and Inman and their parting. It opens with Ruby dealing with the horse, Ralph, and using physical cues to control him; then the action moves to the physical needs of Ada at night in bed, to an aborted attempt at kissing, and finally a proper embrace for the lovers. The action is calm and measured: mending fences, bartering vegetables, making a scarecrow, and doing one's hair. Inman's letter creates action and interest; we recognise Ada's confusion at his words, and the distance of time and experience between them seems unbridgeable at this point, as we know from the last chapter how things are with Inman.

The narratives are geographically and thematically far apart, though the device of the letter draws them into a relationship. But there is still a huge contrast between them, as Inman faces repeated threats of death and at times expects to die; and Ada calmly carries out everyday tasks.

The story of Shining Rocks is detailed and it also expresses some of Inman's proximity to the Cherokee culture that Ada does not possess. It is a key factor in later chapters, as, to more than one character, it will seem the only escape. We have in the last chapters witnessed Ada's gradual acceptance of the ways of the mountain and its people, but here, in her remembered response to Inman's story, she is dismissive: 'Well, that was certainly folkloric' (p. 242).

Ruby and her influence have engendered great change in Ada. Placing the flashback at this juncture in the narrative is a timely reminder of the weaving together of Ada's and Inman's lives, which adds impetus to the narrative, moving it towards an ending that brings them together again.

The scarecrow wearing her mauve dress is physical evidence of Ada's transformation; the bolt of material her father could afford to buy her now has a practical application: to scare birds away from crops. Her identity is transformed, and even Ruby approves.

The context of the war is revisited; photos of men before they leave are 'bristling with weaponry' (p. 237) – **ironically** so, given our knowledge of some of the battles in Inman's memory, as well as the cruel fates of both soldiers and fugitives.

? QUESTION

How important is Ada's social background to her actions and the reactions of those around her?

GLOSSARY

227	**the snake for a new pasture fence** a metal wire to be followed when laying a fence
228	**hasp** metal bolt
231	**shuck** informal clothes
	umber brown coloured
235	**hemp lanyard** thick rope or cord
237	**Tartarean frown** an evil frown
	ambrotype, tin-type, calotype, or daguerreotype early forms of photography
	bowie knives stout hunting knives, named after Jim Bowie (c.1796–1836), who died at the Battle of the Alamo
	forage caps soldiers' caps
240	**potsherds** fragments of broken pottery
243	*North American Review* a news journal covering literature, politics and international news, published in Boston
	Southern Literary Messenger published in Richmond, Virginia, a magazine devoted to 'every department of literature and the fine arts'

CONTEXT

The Dial (1840–4), another publication mentioned in Chapter 10, was edited by Emerson for two years; the purpose of the periodical was 'to furnish a medium for the freest expression of thought on the questions which interest earnest minds in every community'.

CHAPTER 11: THE DOING OF IT

- Inman follows the slave's map to the mountains.
- He meets a goat woman who gives him directions, food, shelter and medicine.
- On his departure, she gives him a picture of a flower.

Inman follows the map from the slave and gets close enough to the mountains to see them, still taking care to hide from the Home Guard. Walking through land with feudal estates and outrageous levels of wealth, he feels that his decision to fight for this social system was wrong. In a forest, which feels ancient, he sees a bent figure that turns out to be an old woman squatting on the ground, setting a trap. He asks her for directions and she asks about his wounds. She promises him food and they walk to her camp.

Goats run up to meet them and she kills and guts one for food. When she asks Inman about the Battle of Petersburg, he is dismissive. She tells how when young she was forced to marry a much older man, but she ran off rather than become his third dead wife. Independent ever since, she has lived off goat and bird meat, gathering provisions from the forest and selling goods and leaflets in nearby towns. Inman buys a leaflet from her.

She is clearly against the slavery of the South. Now Inman confides all of his feelings about his part in the fighting, the pity he felt for the enemy, and the need he has to be close to the rhythms of nature. The goat woman makes him some medicine for his wounds. Inman tells her about his feelings for Ada and spends a few days resting.

One day when he wakes she is not there. When she returns she offers to pay for the food and care, which she refuses. As he departs she gives him a picture of a blue flower.

COMMENTARY

This chapter represents another quiet and nurturing moment in Inman's journey. He wants to be closer to the country he knows, where he imagines people will 'offer less impediment' (p. 250). Happy Valley is **ironically** described as 'foul', and it makes him ill that he has been fighting for a social system made up of hierarchy and dire poverty. He has true contact with only one character in this chapter and from her he receives all he needs to recuperate, plus timely advice and philosophy.

The precise narrative description of Inman ensures that we understand his lack of solidity. He feels he is becoming a 'veil or mist' (p. 251); substantial artefacts are around him but he is not one of them; and the goat woman also seems to merge into her surroundings: 'not much but its head and shoulders showing above a bed of tall bracken … Not coot but crone' (p. 253). But the goat woman, as Ruby did earlier, metamorphoses into a palpable and vividly described woman: 'her cheek skin glowed pink and fine as a girl's' (p. 253).

The brief interaction between the two characters begins with some defensiveness and ends in respect and warmth. They have a careworn toughness in common and both agree that 'Scarcity's

www. CHECK THE NET

For a discussion by Barry Lopez of the place of landscape in American narratives, visit **www.lopezbooks. com** and click on Lopez's introduction in Articles.

much more the general bearing of life' (p. 263). Inman's deeper reactions to the war are explored in conversation with someone far removed from the rigours and pain of the battles. Her eyes are 'wells of kindness despite all her hard talk', and we hear him recounting his 'shame' at killing the 'downtrodden mill workers of the Federal army' (p. 265). In contrast is the humane killing of the billy goat: 'The goat and the woman stared intently off toward the distance as if waiting for a signal' (p. 258). A tender respect for nature and its small details also takes us closer to Inman's true character as he talks of the 'berries ripening and birds flying' and the cheer they bring him (p. 266). We hear again of his alienation from life; he appears to be searching for the codes that the goat woman has access to.

The goat woman's philosophy is heartening in the comfort she gives him: 'That's just pain … It goes eventually' (p. 267). Frazier depicts her offering hard-won wisdom: 'just recollecting pleasures long ago is pain enough' (p. 267).

Inman's love for Ada receives indirect attention in this chapter as he tells how 'he loved her and wished to marry her', even though he is 'galled in body and mind' (p. 268). Again the goat woman's proximity to nature and his own separation from his usual world allow him to explore his inner wants and needs.

The context of slavery and its place in the war receives attention too, and the question posed by the narrative – 'was it worth all the fighting …?' (p. 264) – reflects an earlier chapter, where Inman had help from the 'yellow slave' (Chapter 9).

Thematically, the extreme hardiness and humanity of the goat woman redresses the balance in the overall picture of Inman's journey, both physical and spiritual, for she acts as an antidote to some of his most keenly felt trauma. She offers Inman some of the wealth of natural resources she knows about, and sets him up again for another stage of travelling.

QUESTION

What types of danger is Inman exposed to on his journey and, conversely, how does he receive comfort?

GLOSSARY

251	**wraith** pale spirit or ghost
252	**toper** drunkard
253	**menhirs** standing stones with mythical significance
	gyred moved in circles
254	**shot tower** tower for making lead bullets
255	**mergansers** large diving ducks
259	**peltry** animal furs
	lath framework of wood sticks
260	**twisted willow withes** twigs
261	**smutched** smudged or dirty
263	**Graham flour** whole wheat flour
	specie coin
266	**winesap** dark red apple
268	**metheglin** alcohol with medicine added
271	**picket** sentry or watchman
	the sentences … were hard to parse a hard language to decipher

QUESTION

Novels about war are many and varied. From your reading of *Cold Mountain*, how central is war as a theme in the novel?

CHAPTER 12: FREEWILL SAVAGES

- Ruby's father, Stobrod, is caught in the trap in the corncrib.
- Ruby frees him, feeds him breakfast and he leaves.
- The women check their tobacco crop and, later on, cook a big meal which Stobrod comes to eat with them.
- Stobrod gives an account of playing his fiddle for a dying girl and plays one of his tunes.

One morning Ruby sees a figure down by the corncrib, and finds it is her father, Stobrod. She releases his arm from the trap but is cynical about his reappearance. He is introduced to Ada; Ruby prepares him breakfast but makes him eat it on the porch while she and Ada eat indoors. Stobrod is living with other outliers on Cold Mountain and they are 'heavily armed' (p. 276).

Ruby sends Stobrod away. Next day the women check their drying tobacco and then make a good meal of venison with vegetables. Stobrod appears from the woods and sits at the table; as Ada has no objection they give him dinner. Then Stobrod gets out his fiddle and tells them how he made it while running fugitive from the war.

The next part of his account is of playing the fiddle for a dying girl. The girl's father was desperate to give her comfort as she died. Stobrod tells how he made up a tune, though unsure of himself, and played this mournful melody, which is now central to all of his playing, 'in the frightening and awful Phrygian mode' (p. 283).

He tells Ruby and Ada that he particularly liked to go into Richmond's taverns and play with 'some genius of the guitar or banjo' (p. 284). Music became a compulsion for him. Ruby is again sceptical but he plays for them nevertheless. The music is spellbinding for both women. When Stobrod finishes playing, however, Ruby is still harsh towards him. Ada is amazed at the turnaround that Stobrod has made in his life through his music.

COMMENTARY

This is a brief chapter but one that contains more than a hint of optimism. This positivity comes to the characters and the reader via Stobrod's reappearance with his fiddle and his music. The women's lives are absorbed in their farm jobs but they are clearly beginning to find life easier as their crops are successful and their food is of a high quality.

Ruby's discovery of Stobrod is **ironic** in that her trap has caught not a wild animal but her own father and a fugitive at that. Stobrod's character has been sharply portrayed so far and here a revision is added. He is the first outlier to return to Black Cove and his 'home' on the mountain, which brings the war closer to this strand of the narrative. We hear little of his war experiences but much of his own personal tussle with the world; this has echoes in Ada's and Inman's respective searches for meaning. Stobrod's playing for a dying girl redresses, to a certain extent, his image as a selfish and feckless father.

Music has palliative and healing properties in this chapter, and Ada hears in Stobrod's playing 'utter conviction in its centrality to a life worth claiming' (p. 285).

CONTEXT

Phrygian mode music has its origins in the ancient city of Phrygia, now part of Turkey. One of the most ancient forms of music, it is based on major keys and, when spanning a whole octave, is the same as playing all the white notes on a keyboard from D to D. It was considered the warlike mode in ancient Greek music.

Ruby feeds her father but is unaffected by any connection between them; she tells Ada: 'he's of little matter to me' (p. 275). His character in this chapter is halfway towards being rehabilitated, but the dry humour of Ruby and even the dying girl is likely to prevent us from identifying fully with him at this stage: 'Best go to it ... Time's short' (p. 283). The reader sees him learning from black musicians in the taverns of Richmond and he is portrayed as dedicated to his growing art, rather than the feudal slave-owning system whose side he is fighting for. We remain ambivalent to his character, yet he brings a fresh element of feeling to the story with his 'curious and dissonant' and yearning tunes (p. 285).

In a similar vein to Inman's encounter with the goat woman, nature is re-established as a harmonious and generous force – particularly so on Cold Mountain, where the perfect timber is found for the violin's body, as well as the snake with its important rattle. Killing the snake, Stobrod must undergo the 'mystic discipline' (p. 279). We hear that the mountain is hiding a band of outliers, which will have relevance for later chapters.

See **Text 2** of **Extended commentaries** for further discussion of part of this chapter.

> **CONTEXT**
>
> Richmond, Virginia, the headquarters of the Confederacy, was the site of many fierce battles, including a fire set by retreating Confederate soldiers at the end of the war.

GLOSSARY	
274	a little withy man a tough and agile man
275	shitheels slang term of abuse with connotations of dirty, ignorant, low-down
279	a sizz and knell a hiss and solemn sound
286	stob a post or stump

CHAPTER 13: BRIDE BED FULL OF BLOOD

- Inman is fed and clothed by Sara, a girl living in a cabin on the mountains.
- Federal soldiers arrive and terrorise Sara while Inman hides.
- Inman follows the soldiers into the forest and kills them.
- He stays a further night, then leaves the next day.

Inman is wandering in a state of confusion on the mountainside, having run out of food. A man is following him who turns out to be a Federal sympathiser; he makes some signals to Inman to work out his allegiances. They speak and the man tells him his own son was killed at Sharpsburg; and Inman says he too was at that battle. They both feel unaffiliated. The man, called Potts, gives Inman directions to a woman's house near by where he can get food.

Inman finds the cabin, which is extremely basic, and a young woman, Sara, comes out and offers to feed him. Her house is sparse and clean, plainly furnished and undecorated; a baby is in a cradle. Feeling dirty, Inman sits at the fire and eats greedily. Inman finds out that her husband is dead and she manages on her own. Inman sees that though only eighteen, she will suffer greatly in the next few years. He offers to help kill her hog and she gives him a pile of clothes that were her husband's. He goes to sleep in her corncrib but Sara comes to fetch him in the night and asks him to sleep next to her. When Inman is in her bed, she cries for a while, and then tells of her husband, John, and their former life building the cabin. Then she sleeps and Inman passes a sad and uncomfortable night.

The next day some Federal soldiers come to the house and Inman hides in the woods until they leave. The men terrify Sara by tying her up, threatening her baby and taking her animals into the forest. Inman frees her and sets off to find the men. When he does they are sitting talking of their homes in New York and Philadelphia. Inman hides briefly in a cave with prehistoric paintings on the walls; he shoots all three men and puts their bodies in the cave. Unhappily, he decides he has to kill the horses too, to prevent them tracking back to him or Sara.

Inman returns to Sara's cabin with the hog, which they butcher straight away. They eat some meat and Inman shaves himself with John's razor. Sara sings to her crying baby a song full of despair; the baby falls asleep to the sound of another gruesome ballad about murder. That night Inman sleeps again in Sara's bed, and next day he leaves after a breakfast of pig brains and chicken eggs.

> **CONTEXT**
>
> Inman feels pity for the Federals whom he must kill to save Sara. In his sense of shame at their deaths, Frazier raises the issue of the mill and factory workers from the north-east, who were cannon fodder for the Federal side.

COMMENTARY

In this chapter Inman both gives and receives succour. Before coming to Sara's house he is walking, half lost and wishing for oblivion, to be 'a dark speck on the clear sky' (p. 288). In fact, throughout the chapter Inman's identity and self-image are key themes. He is cool when Potts gives him coded messages, saying, 'I'm not HOA or anything else' (p. 289). When the man adds that he has lost a son at the Battle of Sharpsburg, this information opens Inman up on his memories of the battle: 'Lots of boys died' (p. 290), thus establishing an equal disdain in both men for the war.

Sara is vulnerable but generous, in spite of having very little herself. Inman senses that her sad fate is waiting, ready to 'drop and crush' (p. 294). She offers him clothes and razors from her late husband, gifts which seem to confer on him some special status. His use of them reinforces the theme of identity: 'he felt he had donned the husk of another life' (p. 296). When he has shaved, Sara confirms he looks 'part human now' (p. 309).

The chapter uses a mixture of domestic interiors and darkness to depict intimate human needs, both Inman's and Sara's, away from the terrors and random cruelty of the war. Shadows and light echo the shaky reality that Inman is observing; he sees Sara in a quasi-religious halo but the outer ring of consciousness is vague: 'Everything in the shadows beyond it was extinguished completely, as if never to reappear' (p. 296).

Inman's revenge on the Federals is presented in a morally ambivalent light; afterwards he feels that 'this might be a story he would never tell' (p. 306). The narrative also contains some sympathy for the Federals, who are 'city boys wary of woods' (p. 305). Warfare and its damage to both sides achieve balance in the understated exchange between Potts and Inman: 'You look worn to a nub' (p. 290).

Frazier reminds us about the topography and ancient history of the mountains, and Inman's adding to the cave paintings later suggests he wishes to place his own mark alongside other ancient traces. Sara's quilt itself is decorated with unfamiliar beasts which remind him 'of how frail the human body is against all that is sharp and hard' (p. 307). Adding his own creatures, Inman seems impelled to make sense of his own half-unwilling actions, either in the war, or in killing these soldiers in the wood.

CONTEXT

The Battle of Sharpsburg took place on 17 September 1862, and claimed 12,000 Confederate lives and 10,700 Federal. This battle led to Abraham Lincoln issuing the Emancipation Proclamation in January 1863, and from then on the war was a struggle about slavery as well as self-government.

QUESTION

What does music such as Sara's singing add to the novel in terms of colour, pathos and depth?

Lastly, Sara's singing is redolent of her desperate loneliness, her strength and need; as with Stobrod's fiddle-playing, the music expresses the pain of the human state and has echoes of history and how for centuries women would have sung 'a lesson in how to live with damage' (p. 310).

GLOSSARY

291	pone of corn bread loaf of bread
292	puncheon a wooden post
299	chestnut mast food for pigs
	stopple stopper or cork
303	brainpans skulls
307	caul fat fold of fat between the stomach and intestines
308	chittlings intestines

CHAPTER 14: A SATISFIED MIND

- Ruby and Ada bring in the apple harvest.
- Stobrod comes to Black Cove and introduces Pangle.
- Stobrod asks if they can stay but Ruby refuses.
- That night Ada spends time on her own and writes to Inman asking him to return.

The women harvest their apples. Ruby goes off to barter some cider, leaving Ada to carry out some farm jobs. The work calms Ada and she finishes quickly. She writes to Lucy in Charleston and expresses her contentment at how altered her life is.

Ada then begins burning some brushwood from a field, settling down to read *Adam Bede*. But she is impatient with the characters in the book, and eventually closes it. Looking at the sky and horizon, she realises that she owns a large tract of land, which she measures by the rising and setting of the sun.

Ada hears voices in the woods and two figures come towards her: Stobrod and a man holding a banjo. The companion is described by Stobrod as 'a Swanger boy, or a Pangle' and 'simpleminded' (p. 320).

He had attached himself to the bunch of outliers that Stobrod belongs to and when he heard any music, would dance and sing along. He has formed a special attachment to Stobrod.

Ruby returns after this account, bringing beef with her. She puts it in the fire to cook and then Stobrod and Pangle play some music. Ada is touched by one song, as it seems hopeful and instructive: 'Coarse as the song was, Ada found herself moved by it. More so … than at any opera she had attended from Dock Street to Milan' (p. 325). One last song is darker in tone, and focuses on death but nevertheless contains sweet and close harmonies. They all eat the beef and Stobrod asks if he and Pangle can come to Black Cove for permanent shelter. Ruby's response is harsh and unforgiving; Ada is softer and points out that this is Ruby's father. Stobrod tells a story about a time he left Ruby to brew liquor on the mountainside. Ruby counters with her version of the same story.

Later Ada spends time alone and looks at the moon and stars with Monroe's old spyglass. One of Stobrod's love songs has made a particular impression on her. She writes down a refrain from the song: 'Come back to me is my request', and puts it in a letter which she addresses to Inman's hospital ward (p. 332).

> **CONTEXT**
>
> Ada's attendance at the opera at Dock Street Theatre in Charleston and in Milan in Italy suggests she has had a privileged lifestyle.

COMMENTARY

A large portion of the action in this chapter is devoted to Stobrod and Pangle. It is a relatively thoughtful episode, another gentle moment in the narrative. The conflicts within the chapter are remembered rather than current ones, between Ruby and Stobrod. Ruby has not only her raw memories to live with, but also a sense of daughterly duty, which is not comfortable for her. Ada tentatively offers advice to Ruby, which reverses some of their usual interaction; and as with the hair braiding, they are seen as more intimate again, as Ruby holds Ada's hand and plays with her bracelet while the music plays.

Ada writes two letters in this chapter; this new layer of narrative technique allows a little more personal space to her own thoughts. To Lucy she writes self-consciously about her life: 'It is amazing the physical alterations that can transpire in but a few months of labor' and tells also of her new happiness, 'somehow akin to contentment'

There are many references to the heavens and stars in *Cold Mountain*; in your opinion, what effect does this have on the atmosphere and/ or action of the novel?

(p. 314). We see some of Ada's inner alterations; this awareness is complemented by her simple one-phrase letter to Inman: 'Come back to me is my request' (p. 332). Ada no longer automatically accepts the literature that she reads, but criticises it for being 'cramped by circumstance' (p. 315). Literature is not relevant, for her life is 'set on such a sure course' (p. 316). The new Ada thinks of land in terms of where the sun sets at different times of the year, and her imagination is not curtailed by the limitations of fictional stories. Ada's watching the stars and the moon links to Inman's looking up at the heavens in previous chapters for guidance and support.

Pangle's story takes us close to the real benefits of the mountain and its people; although of very little intellectual ability, he appears to survive just by knowing 'every slit and chink' (p. 321) of the mountain. He lives as an animal and sleeps under the trees eating whatever he can find. His intimacy with nature echoes that of Ruby and the goat woman.

Although the lives that Stobrod and Pangle have led are reminders of how hard it is on the mountain, and will be echoed in the coming chapters, at this stage we are likely to see nature as generous rather than inhospitable. As with Stobrod's often discordant music, the roughness of life, 'cold and stormy', is also alleviated by a chorus with a 'deep place of concord' at its heart (p. 326). This healing music leads Ada to write to Inman and express her real feelings. Such an admission creates further expectation of a hopeful ending for the reader, although we are **ironically** aware that he is no longer in hospital and has been through many dangers since he himself wrote.

The lovers' lives are running half parallel; we are aware that Inman is nearing the mountain, but their respective versions of what is possible are discordant; at this stage we may be concerned that the couple might not match in time or understanding.

GLOSSARY		
312	pomace	apple pulp
	maul	heavy hammer
314	hackerd	a rough tool
315	sere	withered

321	Roman and Jute, Saxon and Angle and Brit tribes from mainland Europe, all of which settled in Britain
329	usquebaugh Irish whiskey flavoured with coriander
	poteen liquor distilled from potatoes
330	Romulus and Remus in the ancient Roman myth two boys, Romulus and Remus, were abandoned by their parents and suckled by a she-wolf; Romulus later killed Remus and founded Rome
331	*Endymion* in a Greek myth Endymion was a handsome youth who was visited by the moon goddess Selene every night

CONTEXT

William Wordsworth and John Keats, English Romantic poets, are both referred to in *Cold Mountain*. The reference to *Endymion* by Keats is another compliment to Stobrod's music and its power for stirring the human spirit. Monroe quoted from Wordsworth's poem 'Composed upon Westminster Bridge' as he and Ada arrived at Black Cove (Chapter 2, p. 50).

CHAPTER 15: A VOW TO BEAR

- Inman buries a dead girl and her grandmother feeds him.
- Travelling on, he comes across three skeletons hanging from a tree.
- A mother bear charges him, going over a cliff to her death.
- Inman shoots the baby bear and eats some of the meat.

Inman is walking fairly steadily through the mountains. He spends a day helping a lone woman bury a dead child; the woman then cooks a large plate of food for him. They manage to say a grace, and the woman shows him a picture of her family with six children. Inman travels on and sleeps in bird houses and coops and reads some of Bartram's *Travels* to calm his mind. Next day he sees signposts and then three skeletons inexplicably hanging from a branch, hung there with plaited hickory wood.

The following day Inman starts to feel he knows the land he is walking through and even puts down a stone on a pile of rocks built by the Cherokee. When he wakes the next morning, he is faced with a mother bear very close to him. Inman realises that she can smell him, and as she moves closer the narrative swaps to a mini-**flashback** in which Inman remembers a series of dreams when he became a bear and roamed the mountains alone. In the final dream he was killed and skinned.

In this situation now, Inman decides to speak to her gently, to ask to be allowed past her without harming her. But she charges and falls over the cliff edge, and is smashed open on the rocks below. Her baby is terrified and Inman dreams momentarily of either giving the cub to Ada, or caring for it himself, but then decides he must save it from abandonment and starvation and so shoots it.

Inman skins and cooks the cub's flesh and, while he waits for it to cook, looks out over the mountains. He remembers a Cherokee word – 'Cataloochee' – for the great vista of mountains he can see (p. 342). He is glad to be approaching home and can even see Cold Mountain. Beginning to feel level again, he wonders whether he might soon feel safe. But eating the bear, he is sad and regretful for what he is doing.

COMMENTARY

This chapter documents Inman's increasing familiarity with the animals and birds of the landscape; but as a counterpoint, there are also necessary and harsh decisions he must make. Inman sacrifices a day's travelling to help a woman with the burial of the last child in her family, and feels responsible for the death of a mother bear and her cub. He is fed as recompense for both actions.

The grieving woman is suffering from dire numbing pain, but her need for inner peace, 'a still mind' (p. 335), means that she feeds Inman despite her lack of instinct for her own survival. Both she and Inman have deep suffering in common and she cannot say anything over the grave, she tells him, because 'Every word in me would come out bitter' (p. 334). The food she feeds him shines luminously and is vividly described: 'the whole plate glistered in the taper light' (p. 335). The sensuous details are set in sharp relief by the drab surrounding scene and the profound melancholy of the encounter.

Inman's travels show how he is attuned to nature; he relies on birds' 'haunts' for some sleep, once in a chicken coop with a smell 'like the dusty remainders of ancient deadmen' (p. 336). On a number of other levels his corporeal and imaginative senses are coming alive in this chapter; Bartram's *Travels*, when he reads it, composes a scene

CHECK THE NET

For helpful background and a link to the text of Bartram's *Travels*, visit the University of North Carolina webpage Documenting the American South at **http://docsouth. unc.edu**

of the mountains he knows, so that he 'reaches' the destination before he physically arrives.

The familiarity with his homeland comforts him as he has 'felt all its seasons and registered its colors and smelled its smells' (p. 337). When he meets the skeletons, his instinct is to touch an arm and to feel the 'grain' (p. 338). He remembers actions and words that belong to the Cherokee culture – further evidence of his cultural familiarisation as he nears home.

Inman has further interaction with death as he is involved in the death of the mother bear and then feels compelled to kill the cub humanely. Killing it compromises his personal morals, for 'it would be on the order of a sin for him to kill one no matter what the expense' (p. 340).

We fear that something approaching the nightmare of becoming a 'dripping red carcass' (p. 340) will be his own fate now that he has broken his own self-ordained ethic, and killed a bear. His mental reckoning before he kills the cub is suggestive of his confused state – he imagines taking it back to Ada, and also a life where he raises a family of bears.

Gloom and elation occur together at the end of the chapter as he feels a 'longing to see the leap of hearth smoke from the houses of people he had known all his life' (p. 342) but also feels himself 'cored out' (p. 343).

Inman's physical world is contracting: 'this was all the world there was' (p. 342), but his ethical dilemmas are no less critical. He is close to his home and relations – even feeling the bears are his 'kin' (p. 341), and that it is 'His place' (p. 343) – yet severe choices are still required of him, as with the dead child and the bears.

The reality of bleak life decisions is made compellingly clear: 'hope itself is but an obstacle' (p. 341). However, a realistic and tender **omniscient narrator** seems to offer some reasoning for killing the bear cub: 'What Inman did, though, was all he could do' (p. 342).

See **Text 3** of **Extended commentaries** for further discussion of part of this chapter.

QUESTION

It could be said that Cold Mountain itself is a character in the novel. Discuss how Frazier uses the forces of nature to restrict, challenge and strengthen the characters.

CHECK THE BOOK

Joseph Campbell's *The Hero with a Thousand Faces* (first published in 1949) carries some useful discussion of the psychological hero figure in literature. In his introduction Campbell examines some typical circumstances and figures within **mythical** literature, citing 'the dark forest', 'the great tree' and rites of 'spiritual passage' as key elements.

GLOSSARY

334	a pod or gall vegetable growth or seed case
	lye soap acidic soap
335	slough mud-filled hollow or bog
	bobwhite North American species of quail
336	bivouac temporary camp
337	squama of fish fish scales
338	rock cairn mound of stones
342	scarp steep slope

CHAPTER 16: NAUGHT AND GRIEF

- Stobrod and Pangle are following a mountain trail with a young outlier from Georgia.
- They discover food left by Ruby.
- Teague and the Home Guard find them.
- Stobrod and Pangle eat with the Home Guard and play music for them.
- Stobrod and Pangle are shot against a tree.

Stobrod, Pangle and a third companion are trekking across the mountains, suffering from eating bad venison the previous night. The third man is an outlier from Georgia with a sad tale of the war. He came to fight with his cousin and when they deserted and reached Cold Mountain, the cousin grew ill and died.

The men find food hidden for them by Ruby under a marked stone; they are not to come to the farm again. From here Stobrod is not sure where to go next, but Pangle tells him the route. The men decide to cook now and walk on later. They build a fire and the young boy from Georgia retreats a distance away into the bushes, troubled by 'the scours' from the bad venison (p. 349). He is still absent when some Home Guard arrive above the clearing. Teague is one of the men, and he orders Stobrod to remain seated. He fires questions at him about a cave where a group of outliers are living, but Stobrod pretends to know nothing about it. Pangle, however, naively tells Teague how to find the cave.

Teague and his men sit and eat, and Pangle falls asleep. Teague then asks Stobrod and Pangle to play some music; although tired and unwilling, they do so. Their music begins discordantly but transforms into a dance, after which they play something more solemn. Teague is complimentary, but tells them both to go over to the poplar tree and they do so, still holding their instruments. The guardsmen prepare to shoot the pair, but Pangle's childish smile puts them off. Teague orders Pangle to put his hat over his face, and Stobrod and Pangle are shot.

COMMENTARY

This chapter deals with the incongruity of two strangely paired men, with their access to higher levels of experience, wishing to found a new community of two 'up near Shining Rocks' (p. 346). This vision of companionship is followed by the casual ease of their deaths.

Through the eyes of Teague, the **omniscient narrator** depicts the men as grotesque: 'Their skin was grey and their eyes looked raw as holes burnt in a quilt top' (p. 350). Where Pangle senses 'warmth and comradeship' (p. 351) in the Home Guard, there is in fact heartless danger; Teague is relaxed and cool in his role; he sits loosely in the saddle with his gun fitting against 'the swell of his thigh' (p. 350). Likewise the violin and banjo cohere into the bodies of Stobrod and Pangle; they are later shot holding them, perhaps as defence against their assailants. They play 'awful old music' (p. 354), thus expressing their culture. The music is **elegaic, foreshadowing** their deaths as well as reflecting the age of bloodshed in which they live.

The guardsmen are well provided for; their food suggests the butchery they have previously undertaken and is sensuously delineated, 'coiled like the bowels of something' (p. 351). In contrast, Pangle is a semi-religious 'sculpture carved in the medium of lard', and we hear from Stobrod that he is 'Gone from the world' (p. 352), which might prefigure his looming death or evoke his ethereal music.

 **QUESTION**

To what extent is the novel about internal or external journeys? What other layers of action exist in the narrative?

Before the Home Guard arrive the setting is silent and colourless, cold and dark. The music Pangle and Stobrod play echoes the metaphoric and actual trail they are on to find safety. Travelling together 'to see what sort of thing they had composed' (p. 353) is perhaps the most rational thing to do with their fugitive existence. In contrast to their messy, almost pointless deaths is the comparative grace of the musical phrasing: 'together they made a complete world' (p. 355).

> **CONTEXT**
>
> Teague represents unrelenting villainy in the narrative, and could be characterised as a force similar to those in psychomachia, an **allegory** about vices and virtues in conflict over the soul of Everyman.

In narrative terms, this chapter shows Teague on the mountain, the geographical focus of the book, so we know Inman is now in greater peril. Teague is now in control of his own narrative, it is not related by another as in earlier chapters, and his menace looms more directly for the reader. He talks in clipped, threatening terms: 'Quit grinning' (p. 356). The characterisation relies on tiny details: 'He … twisted up a slight shade of meaning with one corner of his mouth' (p. 351). When deciding to kill the men he looks 'off in the distance as if trying to remember something' (p. 355).

The deaths themselves are delineated in slightly surreal terms, with Pangle's grin detaching the reader from the real threat he faces. The bullets go through their bodies as if through 'meat', echoing the sausages in the Home Guard's saddlebags. Nature also is hurt by the murders: 'wood chips flew from the great poplar trunk' (p. 356).

Higher aims are revisited in this chapter, as we see Stobrod and Pangle trying to find their own Shining Rocks community. Inman too has links to this Cherokee world, the ancient messages of the forest and mountain, so that the forward spiritual thrust of the narrative remains in spite of the deaths.

> **GLOSSARY**
>
> 349   scours diarrhoea

CHAPTER 17: BLACK BARK IN WINTER

- The boy from Georgia tells Ruby and Ada about the deaths of Stobrod and Pangle.
- They feed the boy before setting off to fetch the bodies.
- They find Pangle's body and bury it.
- Stobrod is still alive and Ruby extracts a bullet from his back.
- They take him to a deserted Cherokee village.

CHECK THE FILM

Anthony Minghella's 2003 film version emphasises Stobrod's paternal role, and lessens our criticisms of his abandonment of Ruby in favour of a warmer character portrayal. What does Stobrod's personal journey contribute to the novel?

The chapter opens with the Georgia boy retelling the story of Teague's men shooting Stobrod and Pangle. Ada and Ruby are sceptical. He tells them he will not return to the mountain but he wants food and another blanket before he sets off for home.

Ruby gives him directions. Ada sees that Ruby is not grief-stricken over her father's death. The women dress in men's clothes for the journey and depart, telling the boy to sleep in the hayloft until he leaves.

The light is gloomy and Ruby pushes them on to reach a set of rocks she remembers from her days foraging in the forest. They stay in the shelter and next morning they wake and find Pangle's body covered in snow, but no sign of Stobrod.

They bury Pangle under a tree, and Ada weeps. She makes a basic cross for the grave head. Ada notices Stobrod sitting up under an overhang of rock, with his fiddle in his lap. They extract a bullet from his back and then make for a long-abandoned Cherokee village. There they choose a hut to move into, put Stobrod inside and build a fire. Ada is downhearted and senses there is more snow to come.

COMMENTARY

The reader is now aware of how much closer the two main protagonists are. The aftermath of Pangle's shooting occupies the women fully and we see their practical abilities. They are depicted as rescuers dressed as men to cope with the elements they will face. The mountain itself is seen initially through the eyes of the boy as an inhospitable place, for 'Every companion he'd had there was now dead in its woods' (p. 358). He also reminds us of the moral baseline, so often blurred in the novel, when he says, 'I don't know what kind of place this is … where people do one another that way' (p. 357). This is an echo of earlier reactions of Inman and Veasey, facing Home Guard violence.

Ruby's apparent toughness resurfaces when she refuses to grieve over Stobrod's death. In contrast are the Georgia boy's own raw feelings over his cousin's body; his actions in placing the body behind the waterfall remind us of the need to make sense of brutality. There are echoes with Inman's earlier moral sense in burying the child and showing tenderness to Veasey's body. In Ruby's belief system, to rest on the mountain is perfect; Ada's antipathy to doing this, believing it to sound 'so informal, like burying a dog' (p. 360), is further evidence of their contrasting lore and values.

Journeys as a theme have new treatment here. The women are filled with 'dread' (p. 362) and we are aware of how relatively easy their life has become. This journey takes them back to Ruby's tough childhood as a forager, and Ada's angle on the trek shows their contrasting lives. She remembers Monroe linking types from nature to the lessons one should learn in life. The trails the women try to follow are now 'a set of points that no longer existed' (p. 364), suggesting moral drifting. However, the women come across arrowheads in an old fireplace and Ada is relieved to decode them as 'Flakes of old hope however slight' (p. 365).

References to prehistory enhance the sense of security in the dolmen with 'chestnut and oak trees that had never been cut since the day of creation' (p. 365). We see Ada trying to make out animal shapes in the light and shadows of the fire, shapes which link back to the images on the quilt in Sara's cabin (Chapter 13).

CONTEXT

In Greek mythology Persephone was the unwilling wife of Hades, who was kept prisoner for half the year in the underworld.

When Pangle is buried, Ada's response is to see his death in terms of the Greek **myth** of Persephone. Ruby's own actions in this scene are tangible measures to relieve pain, but she is adamant that the best herb for healing has left the forest because people are 'not worthy of healing' (p. 371). Her tender respect is for Pangle's life – she touches him 'as if to stamp him with the badge of a like outcast' (p. 368).

The action of the chapter is perceived largely through the eyes of Ada, and so the reader experiences her disorientation. Out on the mountain, Ada faces raw emotions; she is fearful of 'loss so total and so soon' (p. 375) when she recalls the stories of the Cherokee before they left on the Trail of Tears. Though protected on the farm, this crucial stage of her maturation must take place. She must order her mind to be 'congruent with where she was' (p. 374). The chapter is full of references to Ada's own sense of personal crisis.

GLOSSARY

364	gudgeon ... pintle	parts of a hinge
365	dolmen	heap of stones suggesting a tomb
371	goldenseal	alkaline woodland plant used medicinally

CHAPTER 18: FOOTSTEPS IN THE SNOW

- Inman is looking for Ada and Ruby on the mountain.
- Snow covers the women's tracks, and Inman is close to despair.
- At the village, Ruby tends to Stobrod while Ada hunts wild turkeys
- Inman and Ada meet.

Inman is close behind the women and we discover through a **flashback** that he is indeed looking for them. He had been to Black Cove expecting a reunion with Ada, and had been told instead that she was on the mountain with Ruby. Before he arrived at Black Cove he had built a large fire, and washed his clothes expecting an emotional reunion. The boy from Georgia gave an elaborate account of the killings, and sentimentalised the story of Stobrod's fiddle-playing.

Inman is ill and weak. He had started to imagine that seeing Ada would give him hope for the future, but now following footsteps in the snow is his only hope. The snow begins again, the tracks start to disappear and as they do so, he weeps.

www. CHECK THE NET
The American Civil War bankrupted most industries in North Carolina, including agriculture. For more information on how the war affected farming, visit **www. ncagr.com** and follow the link to Agricultural History.

Back at the village, Stobrod is in a fever and Ruby tends to him. She sees some wild turkeys and sends Ada off with a gun to shoot some. Inman hears the shot and knows it is close by. Ready to shoot, he manages to make out a figure training a gun on him. At last he sees it is Ada. As she doesn't answer, he begins to wonder if she is just a trick of his imagination, brought on by fatigue. For Ada, the figure is a stranger.

Inman tells her he is not going to let her go and drops his gun. He understands her suspicion and half decides to walk away. But she recognises him and orders him to leave with her. As they walk she talks about picture she had seen with her father years before in Europe, and her self-assurance comforts him.

COMMENTARY

The storylines converge in this chapter, and with them various themes of love, hope and survival. The reunion has a false start with Inman's 'imagined scene of homecoming' (p. 381).

CHECK THE NET
There are many allusions to pilgrimage in the novel, and *The Pilgrim's Progress* by John Bunyan would be useful background for an understanding of journeys to moral righteousness. *The Pilgrim's Progress,* an **allegorical** work, was published in 1678 and quickly became a 'bestseller' for its time. A helpful version of the work is on **www.bartleby. com** – follow links to John Bunyan.

Inman feels Ada could save him but his **alter ego**, a 'dark voice … in Inman's mind' (p. 384), suggests he will be too damaged to have a normal life. When he loses their tracks under the snow he is truly crushed. The theme of journeys, however tortuous and hopeless, is forcefully emphasised in this chapter as the characters' routes collide. Both physical and psychological wholeness is at stake, especially for Inman.

Inman is better prepared for what may transpire when he meets Ada again, whereas she has taken on a new **persona** for a while, as a hunter and a man. They are in fact, with heavy **irony**, armed when they face each other: 'weapons glinting hard light into the space between them' (p. 390). Reality is hard to pin down for both: he is half ready to be tricked by the spirit world and wonders if Ada is just a dream; she appears the stronger and he the weaker.

But now, to Ada, he is possibly the worst kind of reality – she too is aware of the stories of madmen lost in storms. The codes and understanding between them are completely adrift as he gestures and talks of love and longing, and she simply says, 'I do not know you' (p. 391). The reader recognises the interminable quality of Inman's journey: he is 'a lone pilgrim going on and on' (p. 379).

He has no choice but to leave, and clearly the covered tracks are figurative of the personal pilgrimages he has made: his previous life is no longer an option for him.

The action of the chapter begins with hope of reunion, and the narrative strands achieve some sort of resolution with Ada taking over Inman's decisions as she leads him back to the village. Inman's knowledge of the Cherokee village and the attendant myth forms another possible 'ending' as he dreams of going into another world through the Shining Rocks. This is an echo of Stobrod seeking the Shining Rocks in order that he might build a new world of two with Pangle.

The spiritual messages of the mountain are evoked throughout the chapter, and as with Stobrod and Pangle, with their dream of another world, we witness characters searching for 'deep faith in right order' (p. 384).

GLOSSARY	
381	muleteer person who drives mules
386	tumplines leather straps for carrying loads attached to the forehead
393	Hunters in the Snow large painting by Pieter Bruegel the Elder (1565) depicting hunters and their dogs on a snowy day, with frozen lakes and winter skies

CHAPTER 19: THE FAR SIDE OF TROUBLE

- Ruby tells Ada she can manage without Inman; Ada disagrees.
- Inman gives Stobrod water and eats.
- Inman shows Ada his copy of Bartram's *Travels* and they talk.
- The next day they go hunting and spend the night together.

www. CHECK THE NET

For an image of Bruegel's *The Hunters in the Snow*, visit **www. abcgallery.com**. The painting now hangs at the Kunsthistorisches Museum in Vienna.

The chapter opens with Ruby, Ada, Stobrod and Inman in a hut drinking coffee. In a quiet moment, Ruby tells Ada that they don't need a man to achieve the future they could have. Ada responds by saying that she wants to be with Inman.

Later on Inman wakes and sees Stobrod lying near by; he brings him water from a stream. He goes to the other hut, and Ruby lets him in. Ada appears beautiful to him, and she puts her hands either side of Inman's torso to gauge his size. Inman eats hungrily and Ruby takes some broth to Stobrod in the other hut. Left alone, Ada and Inman are awkward but he shows her his Bartram's *Travels* and explains its significance. He reads a page at random and is embarrassed to find it is about sex.

Inman goes to scour the pans in the creek. Back in the hut he wants to hold Ada, but cannot. They talk about the letters they have written but Ada misses out her last note to him. Inman tells Ada he wants to marry her but cannot expect her to take him on in this state. He reminisces about the time he first saw her in church and says there is no way to recover wasted years. Ruby interrupts the pair and Inman goes off to sleep in the hut with Stobrod. In their hut, Ruby shows her jealousy over Inman. The women decide they will take Stobrod home to recover.

Next day Ada and Inman go hunting together and she explains that Ruby must never be treated as a servant. They find some goldenseal, the herb that Ruby wants to heal Stobrod. They see an arrow in a tree trunk and decide they will come back to visit the spot in years to come.

When they return to the village, Stobrod is awake and Ruby treats him with the goldenseal. The women plan the future for Black Cove and Ruby falls asleep leaning against Ada. Later Ruby decides she must sleep near Stobrod and care for him that night. Ada goes to the other hut, where Inman is asleep. She undresses and the pair finally lie together, alone.

Some hours later they begin to talk about the past but Inman is selective about his war stories and the walk home. He tells her of the goat woman and her philosophy, and they discuss the future.

COMMENTARY

The physical space of this chapter is contracted into small movements and deeds: keeping warm, sleeping, eating. There is interplay between the specifics of life in the woods and the broad

QUESTION

How in your view are the values and ethics of the American South, Cherokee culture and Europe contrasted in *Cold Mountain*?

vista of the future, which is transformed into a number of versions at the hands of Ruby, Ada and Inman.

The past receives attention when Inman and Ada speak, but with significant omissions of war and the suffering Inman has experienced there. He wants to rebuild his ethics, and 'judge himself by another measure' (p. 419). The new reality of their personalities has to be accounted for by both, so that explanations and justifications dominate their interaction. The dialogue shows them talking haltingly at first and recounting their letters to each other, which helps to connect past and present selves by creating a sequence in their behaviours. Ada feels it is an opportunity to 'rewrite even a shard of the past' (p. 405).

They need to fashion some kind of status quo for themselves, and Ada feels 'an entirely other order prevailed from what she had always known' (p. 404). Much of this interaction is narrated indirectly, with an **omniscient narrator** adding the characters' inner feelings; we are thus aware of their different angles on the future.

There is **irony** and humour in the coincidental erotic scenes from Bartram's *Travels*, but they too are an idealised version of human intimacy, and only serve to arouse interest for Inman in reclining 'on the hemlock bed with Ada beside him' (p. 403). However, the silence between the two suggests embarrassment rather than closeness. Physical intimacy and love are experienced at several points in the chapter: when Ada feels Inman's breadth, when she hold Ruby's hand, when Ruby falls asleep against her and both times when the lovers are alone.

> **?** **QUESTION**
>
> Examine the gender restrictions and overlaps used by Frazier. What do you feel they add to the plot?

Discordant elements arise: Ruby too is given a voice and tells Ada: 'we can do without him' (p. 396). Seeing Inman's kit in his hut, Ada is faced with the man she hardly knows: 'The Outlier, His Kit' (p. 415). Another fantasy narrative is created by Ada and Inman of Cherokee lives in the village. And as they talk later, they narrate their stories so that 'they can move forward paired' (p. 417).

Inman feels he is 'disordered' and 'ruined' (p. 406), and by the end of the chapter the 'possibilities narrow down moment by moment' (p. 421). The chapter is laying out ground for a future where Ada must live without Inman; we see her planning next year's work with Ruby, as well as discussing how grandchildren will visit the arrowhead and talk of their predecessors.

CONTEXT

The Isle of Prospero is the setting for Shakespeare's *The Tempest,* and Ada's use of it is indicative of her Western education; Arcady too (from the real Greek region Arcadia) is a pastoral idealised setting in Shakespeare and other classical literature. Ada's reference to them tells us that she feels this world up on the mountain is far more substantial than her Charleston background, which is 'some made-up place' (p. 402).

GLOSSARY

402	Arcady or the Isle of Prospero imaginary places, poetic settings separate from reality
415	mica silicate crystal rock which can retain light and heat
417	censer container for burning incense

CHAPTER 20: SPIRITS OF CROWS, DANCING

- The snow is melting and the lovers make final plans for Inman to go to Virginia, and the women to return to Black Cove with Stobrod.
- They set out, Ada and Ruby in front, and the men behind.
- Teague and the Home Guard appear to face the men.
- Inman sends Stobrod away on the horse and kills several men, including Teague, but is killed by a young boy.
- Ada hears the shots, turns back and finds Inman dying.

As the snow melts Ada and Inman are planning their future, which will mean Inman leaving for Virginia and crossing to the Federal side to give himself up and wait for the end of the war. They are both aware that the war is drawing to a close, so this will be only a temporary arrangement.

Stobrod is better, and after five days in the village they decide to leave, split into two parties in case they meet Home Guard. It hurts Inman to see Ada go; he puts Stobrod on the horse, Ralph, and they set off. The men pass Pangle's grave, and shortly afterwards horsemen appear, spreading out behind them. Stobrod recognises Teague among the men. The Home Guard have two dogs, and Inman immediately strikes the horse to send it off with Stobrod. Inman shoots one man and the dog closest to him. In the ensuing chaos horses charge and men struggle to keep control;

Inman shoots another guardsman. Inman kills Teague and dispatches a guard lying injured on the ground. He sees the last rider, a boy, hiding and calls to him, trying to coax him out from behind a tree. The boy falls off his horse and prepares his gun. A shot goes off and Inman is seriously injured.

Ada hears the shots and runs back. She finds Inman lying separately. She tells him not to speak and he dreams of perfect worlds with all seasons taking place, fruitful landscapes, and crows or their spirits in trees.

COMMENTARY

The last chapter contains the death of Inman and comprises a final journey for the two men as well as some revisiting of significant stages as they start their walk home. They see Pangle's grave and Stobrod reminds us of the boy's naivety, 'wanting nothing but warmth and music' (p. 426). Passing the pond, Inman wonders if the trapped duck has flown away or died, a thought which **foreshadows** his own death.

Splitting Inman and Ada for the last six hours' trek home briefly recreates their divided story strands. The expectation of Inman's journey 'Over the Blue Ridge' (p. 423) gives the reader a sense of future potential. The narrative generalises their choices and tells us that many other couples had 'reached identical conclusions' (p. 422). These choices are narrow and all fraught with risk; **ironically**, the Shining Rocks 'land of peace' (p. 423) option, as their last resort, is closest to what they achieve as Inman slowly dies.

Teague and his men have their last appearance in the novel. The scene where Inman is Teague's adversary, facing him, has a different tenor to other times when Teague is the persecutor. Inman is fully aware of his choices, and the clipped phrase 'No sense waiting' (p. 427) depicts his clear thought patterns. Stobrod is again saved, this time by Inman, and the panic which follows sets Inman into an even more definite frame of mind: 'No wall to get behind. No direction to go but forward, no time but now' (p. 427). He quickly and dispassionately kills several men, but saves his sympathy for the final boy, whom he 'hoped not to have to shoot' (p. 429). This

> **CONTEXT**
>
> A fair number of Confederate deserters crossed the mountains and entered service in the Union army; estimates vary, but a figure of four thousand has been suggested.

QUESTION

How are visual distance and separation used in the novel to determine how the reader views the characters? Think particularly about the final tableau, where the reader is directed to withdraw from the action.

QUESTION

Inman is often associated with images of animals and birds. What does this use of symbol add to the novel as a whole?

ambivalence, together with the humane touch, echoes other times he has chosen not to kill, resulting in danger to himself.

The description of Inman chasing the boy feels playful: 'just a man on a mount and one afoot chasing each other in the woods' (p. 430), which might remind us of Inman's games with Swimmer on the plateau. The extreme vulnerability of the boy, 'white in the face … his hair cropped close' (p. 431), belies the eventual outcome in which Inman dies and the boy hardly knows how it has happened. After surviving the serious dangers he has been exposed to on his journey, Inman is killed almost by accident, and by the least of his assailants. The irony of this event might be described as ponderous, yet our knowledge of Inman's character and values adds precision to it.

Some order is rediscovered in the **tableau** of Ada holding Inman while he dies. Inman's 'bright dream of a home' (p. 432) has echoes of Shining Rocks, Black Cove in its fruitful months, and the various reveries which the lovers indulged in back in the Cherokee village. Crows, so often observed and admired in the novel, resurface; but this time they are spirits, and we gather from this that the final stage of Inman's personal journey has been reached. He is now closer to spirits of birds in 'the upper limbs' (p. 432) of white oaks than the ground he lies on.

The final paragraph renders the reader an observer, and focuses also on the precise detail of the lovers' respective postures. We recognise a powerful present intimacy and imagine a 'conceivable history where long decades of happy union' are possible (p. 432).

GLOSSARY	
423	catamount mountain cat
430	drawing a bead pulling a trigger

EPILOGUE. OCTOBER OF 1874

- A family which consists of Ada, a nine-year-old girl, Ruby, Reid, three boys and Stobrod assemble for a meal.
- It is their last autumn meal outside, a tradition they have upheld since the war.
- After they eat, Stobrod plays his fiddle, and the children play.
- Ada reads the myth of Baucis and Philemon.

CONTEXT

In the Greek myth of Baucis and Philemon, an old couple were rewarded for their kindness to Jupiter with a promise that they could live together for ever – on their death they became two trees, an oak and a linden, growing side by side, intertwined.

Ada's story continues; we are informed that she still lives with Ruby, the boy from Georgia – Reid – and their family of three boys. We learn that Reid decided to stay and became Ruby's husband after two years of working on the farm.

Ada herself appears as a lone woman setting a table for the last picnic of the year. She loves all times of the year but especially the autumn. Ruby and a girl aged nine appear and it becomes clear that this is Ada's daughter. They are carrying food to the table. Finally Stobrod comes to the table with a pail of milk.

After they eat, Stobrod plays a tune and the children play and run. The girl sings in a strong voice; and afterwards Ada reads from the myth of Baucis and Philemon.

QUESTION

The final scenes of the book merge a number of cultural references to music, from both Scottish and bluegrass traditions, with a Greek myth about the permanent nature of true love and the suffering that follows loss. In your view, how much does the novel recycle old treatments of the stories of love and commitment, and how much does it create new ones?

COMMENTARY

The scene opens by drawing together both characters and themes. Ada sees Ruby and Reid in the field, their hoes seeming to work 'the secret engines of earth' (p. 433), an image which depicts them as types who fulfil a role in nature. Venus, goddess of love, gradually appears in the sky; there is a sense that pain and loss have been replaced by settled methods and regularity. Ada still looks for metaphors in nature, yet is hardy enough to know the cycle of the seasons 'had neither inauguration nor epilogue' (p. 434). Ruby's character retains its earthiness; 'A foot in the back' in her marriage is as helpful as a 'hug' (p. 433). Even the previously shiftless Stobrod has his place, milking the cow and contributing to the meal and entertaining afterwards with music.

CONTEXT

Ovid (43BC–AD17) was a Latin poet, born in Italy. One of his major poems was *Metamorphoses*, written in fifteen books, a collection of mythological tales involving transformation, such as the story of Baucis and Philemon.

www. **CHECK THE NET**

You can read a translation of Ovid's *Metamorphoses* online at **http://classics.mit. edu/Ovid**; the story of Baucis and Philemon can be found in Book 8.

QUESTION

In your view, how ideal or realistic is the epilogue in comparison to the rest of the narrative?

Harmony and discord are mixed in the scene: the choice of music mixes good and evil as Stobrod plays 'Angel Band' on 'the devil's box' (p. 435). Nature has damaged Ada by taking off the end of her finger in an accident, but this too now appears entirely congruous, for it is 'the way the ends of people's fingers were meant to look' (p. 436).

The mood in the epilogue is static in terms of setting, but in contrast, as the family members gather one by one, there is a cumulative effect of generations and blood ties. A new tradition has been formed by Ada creating her own rite in their calendar. She continues to use her education from her life with Monroe to read from Ovid, but the significance is now appropriate to her own situation without Inman. 'Winning back' her story in this way rebalances the overall thrust of the novel, where so many of the mini-stories have ended harshly, implying life is random and cruel, not ordered and positive. Here, however, the farm is flourishing, the evidence being the food on the table, which echoes Inman's own final dream of plenitude on the mountain. The girl is expressing, via music, her relation to the world and the outer reaches of human reality: 'Bear me away on your snowy wings' (p. 435), yet she cheekily tosses her stick in the fire, as Inman might have done with his hat. Finally, both women, previously motherless, are now mothers.

Ada and Inman achieve a form of indirect **apotheosis**, being linked to a myth in which two lovers turn into a tree intertwined at the trunk but with two different sets of leaves.

GLOSSARY

435	**Bonnie George Campbell** a traditional Scots song in which a warrior sets off on his horse but never returns and his wife must bear their baby alone
	Angel Band a traditional bluegrass song about a journey towards death

EXTENDED COMMENTARIES

TEXT 1 – CHAPTER 6: ASHES OF ROSES, PP. 135–8

From 'On the party's final night …' to 'He had been walking backward, not wishing to be shot in the back.'

Immediately before this account, Ada and Ruby are contentedly reading Homer's *Odyssey* and Ruby has dismissed the story of a man who is in a 'swineherd's hut drinking and telling tales' (p. 134), as it sounds rather like her own father, Stobrod.

Ada's account of the lavish party reaffirms our picture of her background as privileged and leisured, and at the same time confirms the terrible perils of war for soldiers who are soon to leave. She comes from a social stratum where her father can afford to buy a bolt of cloth for just one dress, and her attitude is limited and unsympathetic; she describes Blount as 'largely witless' and 'a vain fool' (p. 135). Here, in spite of the jolly party atmosphere and flirtation, the facts of death lurk under the surface of even the most sumptuous gathering.

The memory of the river is presented as outside reality and is contracted to basic shapes: 'The normal qualities of the landscape were altered beyond recognition, distilled to strange minimal parts, simple as geometry' (p. 136). The graphic lines present to the reader a pared-down version of nature where feelings are concentrated and intense. Although ostensibly Ada's words, the early narration is cool and detached to reflect the separation of Ada from the plight of the departing soldiers.

The pace slows as Blount becomes bogged down in grandiose stories. The point of view becomes firmly Ada's as she experiences a 'flush of tenderness' seeing the tears on his face (p. 137). We recognise in the way her 'throat closed against the words' that are 'unutterably false' the woman who is unable to flirt or carry out vacuous chatter in Inman's company at church and at the Christmas party at Monroe's. She deals more in terse phrases than effusive outpourings, and the silent code she chooses here allows Blount to blurt out his honest fears. Blount's emotions run counter to the bravado expected from soldiers, and Ada's silent support allows us to see her in a more tender light. Though she can be harsh and

CHECK THE FILM

Anthony Minghella's 2003 film makes extensive use of light, particularly to show contrast between the danger of outdoor settings and indoor, domestic interiors with an atmosphere of safety.

factual, she is honest and uses physical language instead: stroking his hand is evidence of her capacity for gentleness.

As Blount and Ada enter the house we are aware of the contrast in light and sound. From the silence on the lake they are thrust into an interior 'ablaze with Argand lamps', 'silhouettes of dancers' (p. 137) waltzing to the music of Gungl and Strauss – all of which signify that the couple have returned to their accustomed social milieu.

Ada's sight of herself in the mirror is a metaphor for sudden self-awareness and indicates her growing confidence, as well as being an echo of her attempt to see the future down the well at the Swangers' farm. Her complicated nature is evident, for it seems she is unused to approving of herself: 'how odd it had felt to win her own endorsement' (p. 138). Ada's character is developing as we see her acting with integrity under pressure. Her social setting is not the sole determinant of her behaviour; socially she is unlikely to follow prescribed rules, a fact that is borne out by her actions in staying at the farm, thus risking disapprobation and spinsterhood.

Ada's account is based on a central **irony**, that Blount's eventual fate is to display a magnificent degree of courage; in spite of his fear that he would bring shame on his family, he is in fact a dogged and glorious soldier even in retreat. This is a small **vignette** of the effects of war on the individual. Ada's angle on his death is not recorded here, but the narrative is framed to indicate her respect for the man with the 'heart of a shopkeeper' (p. 137).

For Blount and Ada the experience represents realisation and self-knowledge: for Blount in terms of his ability to be brave in war, for Ada the sudden recognition of her own confidence and good looks. The final phrases bring history and battles into sharp juxtaposition with the facts of death. The choice not to be 'shot in the back' (p. 138) suggests the personal ethics of the man who had wept for fear that he would bring shame on his family. Blount represents some accepted values about war and the defence of one's culture, while Ada too is true to her own nature, not bowing to taboos or social mores. Blount's death is evidence of the waste of war, echoing some of Inman's battle experiences, and the reader accepts the wider social implications for men and women and the expectations on them.

CONTEXT

Joseph Gungl (1810–89) was an Austro-Hungarian musician and composer famous for his fluent waltzes and dance music; Johann Strauss the Younger (1825–99) was at the time the most prominent composer of fashionable waltzes. Gungl and Strauss both travelled around America with their touring orchestras.

TEXT 2 – CHAPTER 12: FREEWILL SAVAGES, PP. 283–6

From 'The music he had made up for the girl …' to '… it is ever possible to find some path to redemption, however partial.'

This passage comes just over halfway through the novel and marks an important stage of familiarisation between Ruby, her reappeared father and Ada. Stobrod has only been to the farm once before; here, although barely made welcome by his daughter, he begins to flesh out into a fuller character for Ada and the reader.

Ruby and Ada are beginning to reap the fruits of their labours, as their relatively sumptuous supper shows, and Stobrod appears with an extra skill to add to their experience of the evening. He has also brought the story of his own transformation into a musician for whom 'the notes just happened effortlessly' (p. 284). The account of playing for a dying girl has been a touching story, and this passage shows the deeper structural significance that music has given to his life: 'to give order and meaning' (p. 284).

The description of the Richmond taverns evokes an unsavoury but creative atmosphere, so that Stobrod's war becomes a time to learn music from 'some genius of the guitar or banjo' in places 'that smelled of unwashed bodies, spilled liquor, cheap perfume, and unemptied chamber pots' (p. 284). The contrast of the stinking taverns with the sublime musical talents serves to remind the reader of social inequalities lurking under the surface of the society the characters move in. Stobrod's character depicts the generality of the spiritual factors at play in the novel as a whole, which is reminiscent of Inman and his sympathy for the hostile Federal soldiers. The hierarchy of value is levelled as Stobrod learns basic lessons about life.

The narrator borrows Stobrod's **vernacular**, recounting how the musicians 'chanted out every desire and fear in their lives as clear and proud as could be' and saying that music has 'meat to it' (p. 284). The characterisation of Stobrod relies on this use of his tonal register; we sense his special excitement as he encounters through music a new set of experiences, culminating in his own proud explanation: 'By now he knew nine hundred fiddle tunes, some hundred of them being his own compositions' (p. 284).

CHECK THE NET

For further insights into the vernacular of the Appalachian mountain people, visit **www.pbs.org** and search for the essay entitled 'Smoky Mountain Speech'.

Ruby's reaction to the **hyperbole** is predictably terse; sceptical about the number, she points out that 'his two hands of fingers had always served his entire need for numerals in all other features of life' (pp. 284–5). Their exchange, while showing conflict between the two, adds humour to the narrative, as grandiose ideas are undercut by simple reality.

Stobrod plays and the action switches from verbal exchange to the auditory immediacy of notes and their patterns. The music carries a profound interpretation, which the narrator shares with us: 'Yearning was its main theme' (p. 285), and in this way Stobrod contributes to the layers of desire in the novel but without speech. Stobrod is seen spinning out the music and using long-bowing notes 'easy as a man drawing breath' (p. 285).

As the music dies away, what remains in the scene is the 'voices of peepers' that are 'sad and hopeful in the face of the coming winter' (p. 285), evoking the paradoxes of human experience and **foreshadowing** trials to come. The 'long silence' that follows creates a pregnant pause in which we sense danger and joy.

Ada and Ruby are listeners for this section of the chapter, taking in the 'sweetness and stridency' of the music (p. 285). In contrast to her acerbic reaction to the earlier boasting, Ruby is 'amazed', yet the tension between father and daughter is spun out after Stobrod finishes playing, as the narrative slows down waiting for her response. Ruby's backhanded and grudging compliment, delivered indirectly through Ada, has its own force: 'he's finally found the only tool he's ever shown any skill at working' (p. 286). In this respect Ruby is seen to accept her father's development, which furthers both her character and the action, but her internal bitterness towards him remains.

QUESTION

To what extent are parenting and nurture important issues in the novel?

Drawing further back still from the emotional clash between father and daughter, we next witness Ada's view of the music; Frazier sketches in another layer of moral significance with reference to a 'miracle' and 'some path to redemption' (p. 286), both of which are fully consonant with Inman's journey and Ada's own. Ada too is becoming more magnanimous. Her biblical references retrieve some of Stobrod's selfish nature as he is recognised to be on his own pilgrimage through life.

Stobrod is given no more dialogue in the chapter, suggesting that his communication through music is the closest he will get to meaningful 'speech' at this point. We are still fully aware of his role in Ruby's abandonment, yet the fiddle-playing scene requires a reassessment of him by both women. If he can be rehabilitated, then the hopelessness of the story might be redressed in favour of happiness.

TEXT 3 – CHAPTER 15: A VOW TO BEAR, PP. 341–3

From 'The bear sniffed more' to '… he decided to append an eighth, regret.'

Before the passage starts, Inman is starting to feel at home in his surroundings. He wakes after a night's sleep to the sound and then the sight of a female bear, accompanied by her cub; she smells Inman and is afraid. Inman has recounted a set of dreams he had in the trenches of Petersburg in which he was himself a bear, roaming 'the green dream mountains … happy and strong' (p. 340). Since these dreams, Inman has felt bears are a kind of talisman, and to kill one would bring him misfortune.

But in this position he has no choice, for Inman knows she is likely to charge him, protecting her cub. He has asked for 'clear passage' (p. 341) and has spoken with respect, but she attacks.

The detail of her movements is clearly mapped 'Like a problem of carpentry where none of the dimensions match up' (p. 341), which briefly detaches the reader from the tragedy of her looming death. The physical effect of the bear's body as she rushes by – 'wet dog, black dirt' – re-engages our senses, and the strange paradoxical beauty as she breaks 'like a great red blossom' (p. 341) helps us see with Inman the aesthetic quality of the real bear: she is 'a … blossom', whereas in his dreams he was a 'dripping red carcass' (p. 340).

However, Inman's ensuing silent expletive has a **bathos** effect and we are drawn back into the present disaster, which the bear's death represents for Inman. After all, this is a sin, to kill a bear, and 'hope itself is but an obstacle' is the philosophical position he reaches straight away (p. 341). The concentrated physical action juxtaposed

 CHECK THE BOOK
There is a perennial theme in American literature of men and women seeking to live in, or travel safely through, the wilderness. Protagonists who wish to live 'free from society' are discussed in Nina Baym's essay 'Melodramas of Beset Manhood: How Theories of American Fiction Exclude Women Authors' in *American Literature, American Culture,* edited by Gordon Hutner (1998).

with profound ethical dilemmas is reminiscent of much of the dual journey he is undertaking: survival of both body and soul.

What follows with the baby bear reinforces the psychological action, for Inman fantasises about taking the cub, crying 'like a human baby', and bringing it into the human world (p. 341). As he considers swapping another reality for the current one, the idealised language shows how unlikely it is to work: 'the bear looking about from this new perspective as bright-eyed as a papoose'. The present reality of his choices is again starkly depicted: leaving the cub to wail and starve or killing it mercifully. The killing of the baby bear has other deeper significances, as if he has killed his own chance of having a child and grandchildren.

Once the killing is done, the narrative reverts to practical issues in tune with Inman's own priorities: it is essential for him to eat. The intervening passage, however, describes his personal landscape coming back into focus; the weather, the colours and shapes are sensuously personified: 'Shadows slid down the slopes' and 'Rags of cloud hung in the valleys' (p. 342), so that the look of the mountains is more attractive to him than the swamps of his earlier wanderings. The contracted image of 'this was all the world there was' (p. 342) has at least two levels of meaning: that of a reverie of being separate and enclosed from the outside world, or of being fiercely loyal to the land he sees. Seeing west 'for scores of miles' swings the description back to scope and grandeur, as does 'waves of mountains in fading rows' (p. 342).

CHECK THE FILM

The 2003 film *Cold Mountain* makes much of the seasons and moods of the North Carolina landscape, as if to reproduce the innate yearning of Inman for his native homeland.

We see in the phrase 'there was growing joy in Inman's heart' (p. 342) that the scenery acts as an antidote to his pain. The landscape gives him a sense of touch, 'thin air on skin', and by the end of this paragraph he has identified 'what for him was homeland' (pp. 342–3). The phrase 'It was to Cold Mountain he looked' (p. 343) has a massive effect, as this has been his goal since he left hospital.

The list of features on the mountain acts as a comforting recitation of familiar sounds, and this echoes previous times when he has used the place names to wind down his mind. It ends with great impact in a two-word phrase: 'His place' (p. 343).

This scene has added a new compelling force and vigour to Inman's journey home, but has conversely set up new conflicts. He is not interacting with characters but instead moral forces such as 'sin'. Killing the bear fits with his pressing need to survive, yet the psychic pilgrimage is as important. Weaving together the opposing perspectives of proximity and distance echoes this tension: 'this was all the world there was' (p. 342) is set alongside looking 'into the little bear's face' (p. 341). Cutting up the bear to cook and seeing the landscape in terms of a 'great slab of streaked meat' might also suggest to the reader the connectedness of each of his decisions (p. 342).

QUESTION

How much is war to blame for the suffering of characters in *Cold Mountain*? What else is at the root of the pain?

PART THREE

CRITICAL APPROACHES

CHARACTERISATION

INMAN

CONTEXT

Given the malevolent environment and adversaries in Inman's journey, it might be fair to wonder why the story never collapses into tragedy. There are many echoes of Greek **myths** in the novel, and often the fatal flaw – or hubris – of the main protagonist in Greek tragedy leads to his downfall and death. A counter-argument might be that the crowded narrative thrust of the novel blunts the Inman story. Tragedy here is generalised, non-specific and seems to affect the whole community, of which Inman is just one representative.

Inman is the principal protagonist in the novel, and reaches a type of tragic culmination at the end. From the start he is depicted returning to the real world from the nether regions of war, and must rebuild his own damaged psyche too. Little of his previous life is sketched in aside from his friendship with Swimmer, his father teaching him how to collect honey from bees' nests, and a decision to leave school. He therefore stands somehow on his own merits. If anything his cultural references are Native American and rural – he knows how to clear fields, how to wield a scythe; he has heard stories and spells from the Cherokee.

Survival is his most pressing issue in the main narrative, but his more profound needs surface as much in the **flashbacks** where, for example, we learn of the time he first saw Ada's neck in church, and of how he bade farewell to her and tried to kiss her. The role which Ada plays in his will to survive is frequently referred to, so that her image and the normality she represents become **totemic** to him.

Inman's pilgrimage includes some exposure to sexual temptation, for example with Lila in Junior's house; seeing the women washing clothes in the river; and, most intensely, the nights spent in Sara's bed. Veasey is perhaps the character who elucidates some of these earthier factors of life in the novel, particularly as he is caught by the siren figures at Junior's house and Tildy at the drovers' lodge (see **Characterisation: Secondary characters**). Inman represents, rather as Odysseus does, a journey towards the expiation of sin: 'a dark monk out awander for the good of his soul, seeking remedy in walking from being fouled by contact with the world' (Chapter 13, p. 290). War and its immorality and the general ethical chaos of the world need to be atoned for, and the reader is frequently directed to connect Inman's state of mind to his ethical choices, as in the killing of the bear and her cub, where he must face a decision that involves 'sin' (Chapter 15, p. 340).

Inman often wants to leave the current world, 'Fly off to some high ridge and perch, observing the bright light of common day' (Chapter 13, p. 288), or feels he is beginning to fade, 'in the process of becoming some mere figment … A traveling shade' (Chapter 11, p. 251).

We see Inman facing immediate dubious choices, whether to lose a day and help the old woman bury the girl, or to kill the Federals to save Sara losing her hog.

The novel has Inman at its centre; along with Ada, he carries half of the character thrust, and probably more than half of any moral weight too. In traditional terms his rebirths – 'To rise and bloom again, that became his wish' (Chapter 9, p. 220) – place him firmly in the role of hero; he also acts as an antagonist to the evil of others, whether it be Veasey's lasciviousness or Junior's cruel depravity. He heals the wounds of others as he goes, is seen to regret sins of the war, and has therefore more of a past to carry with him, which introduces elements of historical context. These serve in some ways literally to consolidate his place in the narrative. For example, his experiences at Fredericksburg are backed up by contemporary accounts of the war; in this sense his substantial soldiering role is a counterweight to the 'personality' we see fade in and out of focus in the story.

As Inman nears Cold Mountain his physical transformation mirrors his emotional journey; his wound is healed, and although he feels 'cored out' (Chapter 15, p. 343), he starts to feel rebalanced and alive.

There is ambivalence in Inman's character; as he travels, his wanderings are punctuated by a number of interactions with other people, but the lone journey always resumes. Inman has weaknesses as well as strengths, as does any hero figure in literature, but there does not appear to be one 'tragic flaw'. His enemies are more a concatenation of circumstances which act either for or against him and, finally, kill him. His humane side is frequently apparent in conversation with Veasey, the goat woman and Sara; in his reaction to the random cruelty of Junior; and in the moments before he is killed by the boy.

> **CONTEXT**
>
> The significance of Inman's name comes into its own during the novel: it is both a universal name, like 'Everyman', and suggestive of inwardness, of someone on a spiritual, inner journey.

 CHECK THE NET

The *Cold Mountain* theme of the expiation of sin has many parallels with *Everyman*, the medieval morality play. For helpful material on morality plays and *Everyman* in particular, dip into **www. luminarium.org/ medlit**

ADA

Much of the structure of *Cold Mountain* is built around parallels, and the character of Ada might be seen as a female version of Inman, plotting her own course through the same period of time but with her own crises and learning to negotiate.

Frazier has woven into her character strands of social behaviour such as gender expectation, which are issues she must tackle as part of her survival. Early on she typifies her class and gender, and relies on others for help and back-up. Although she is internally a solitary character, she is dependent on others for direction. Inman's journey is in contrast a sole one. Her conflicts are physical – living without her father, eating enough to exist – as well as psychological; that said, part of the framework she must alter to survive is her intellectual and abstract nature. We see her realising that this may not reflect enough of the world she wants for herself: 'She wished all the people of the story to be more expansive' (Chapter 14, p. 315). This recognition is a key marker in her development.

Her early characterisation functions around opposites; for example we meet her alone, fighting a rooster, but the elevated background she belongs to is quickly sketched in. Ada's intellectual depth is immediately striking; she is happy to speak in rarified codes and at the outset requires respect in return. Hence Inman suggesting she is prickly, 'Like grabbing up a chestnut burr' (Chapter 3, p. 78). Likewise, she speaks to Mrs McKennet in lordly terms of the war; the way in which she is rebuffed by the woman and in other interactions with Ruby – 'Don't act so proud' (Chapter 6, p. 133) – ensures that her character is seen through the eyes of other, more grounded people, and we are likely therefore to develop a detached humour in our view of her. Indulged by her father and with references to literature and **myth** marking her early milieu, the **irony** of her new life is present from the opening pages.

Ada does, however, learn humility and develop warmth as a character; this is shown in chapters where she and Ruby are engaged in the farm work; for Ada, recognising the 'luminous quiver' (Chapter 6, p. 134) of nature is a turning point. Her ability to work with nature marks her progress on her journey, as does putting her books aside to work. She grasps the significance of touch and

CONTEXT

Ada's reading includes some topical and literary magazines and journals of the time, such as the *North American Review* and *The Dial*.

tangible sensuous elements in life: the closing chapters have her touching Inman to gauge his weight and health; thus her intuitive earthy reactions and interactions with Inman and Ruby have great significance for our view of her.

The later characterisation of Ada as Inman dies, and nine years later in the epilogue, is relatively serene and detached; the stories are told in general terms. She is the 'woman', he the 'man'; likewise in the epilogue she is linked to a myth of a woman and man remaining in a true loyal relationship, and is seen observing others such as Ruby and Reid – 'Ada still found them clasping each other at the oddest moments' (Epilogue, p. 433) – rather than being at the forefront of the action herself.

RUBY

To balance the character of Ada and her genteel values, Frazier has created a highly successful antidote in Ruby. She makes an unexpected entrance into Ada's world and rights its physical hardships in favour of an earthy appreciation of how the world really ticks. The character of Ruby develops perhaps the least out of any of the *Cold Mountain* characters because she seems somehow to be whole from the start. Her experience as a child in the woods appears to have prepared her for any trial, but her hardbitten toughness also belies her sensitivity, which is brought out by her close friendship with Ada. Ada even suggests a hair-plaiting competition as a way of allowing Ruby some contact, 'both intimate and distant' (Chapter 10, p. 233), and the women play with each other's hands and Ada's jewellery when listening to Stobrod's music, which suggests contact is needed by both. Ruby has a soulful side which comes out occasionally, as when the women read books and when she talks to the heron.

Ruby ends the novel as she began, belonging to the earth. Barefooted when Ada first meets her, by the close she and Reid seem to be working 'the secret engines of earth' (Epilogue, p. 433). Her inner demons are largely to do with Stobrod. The healing of their relationship is a rocky road, with wry comments and outright rejection from Ruby along the way, but it is achieved in the end. Ruby brings humour and lightness to Ada's worthy and moralistic take on reality; she debunks Ada's pretensions: 'This business of

? QUESTION

Ada and Ruby might both be considered to be oddities in terms of the world they live in. How successful do you find Frazier's characterisation of them? Do they throw up questions about the role of women?

carrying hats halfway around the world to sell made no sense to her' (Chapter 10, p. 234).

Ruby insists on respect from Ada, and refuses to empty Ada's night jar; likewise she insists on treating Ada fairly too. She shows some jealousy when Inman comes into Ada's life, for she is sure they can manage without him. If Ada and Inman are the male and female protagonists in the novel, Ruby is the most significant other **persona**. Her contribution to the action and her characterisation ensure that the reader is closely aware of concrete problems and the business of life.

THE FATHERS
MONROE

The fathers in *Cold Mountain* are reminders of the backgrounds of the two female characters. Monroe is an establishment man, who, with his respect for traditional Western European values, has fed Ada with a version of life which she must modify. Monroe has in his own right been a brave man, but we see him in his latter years, with a weak chest and a philosophy taken from Emerson that seems outdated and too intellectual for his new life. He hardly fits into the Cold Mountain community and is ridiculed, then humoured, by his congregation. The **flashback** detailing his courtship and later marriage allows him his own voice in the book: 'When I rose again, it was with the determination that my life was now at your service' (Chapter 8, p. 194).

But Monroe has overprotected Ada, and the result is clear in her precious attitude, which leaves her vulnerable to the vagaries of real life until Ruby appears. He has fed her with trips to Europe, with literary stories, philosophy and **myth**, but she cannot cook for herself or grow vegetables. He is an idealist, and quotes Wordsworth at will; his pure philosophy gives Ada strengths – 'Monroe had a book wherein you could look up the types' (Chapter 17, p. 363) – but is also a drawback as she searches to fashion her own philosophy.

STOBROD

Stobrod begins with little substance and achieves status by the end of the novel. He starts out as an **anti-hero**, someone who has enlisted for want of something better to do, leaving his daughter

CHECK THE BOOK

Dip into Emerson's *The Conduct of Life* (1860); of particular interest is the Fate section, which elaborates on his ideas on the links between nature, man, agency and fate.

alone in the process. Yet later he might be said to replace Monroe in Ada's household, as an elder and a grandparent.

Stobrod belongs to his own feckless and shifting world, but has another power highly valued in the novel, that of music. He is depicted as rough and coarse; he speaks and manipulates mostly for his own gain, but is transformed by the music he plays into someone who creates a 'complete world' (Chapter 16, p. 355). Stobrod makes the characters around him react either in disgust and shame – like Ruby, who cannot take him and his claims seriously – or in wonder at his skill.

Stobrod almost dies and is saved twice in the novel; caught by his daughter stealing corn and by Teague twice in the mountain, his survival suggests that the irredeemable can also be reborn into responsibility and stature.

His boasting injects humour into the novel, as we see the gap between what he claims and what is likely to be true. He is a rich counterpoint to the overweening care of Monroe for Ada as he has abandoned Ruby more than once; his own spiritual journey is constructed to show him asking for forgiveness, begging for food and shelter and being saved by his daughter and her friends. As an anti-hero Stobrod is permitted to survive, and he brings his own resources to the life of the post-war survivors. When he plays and sings he can balance the devil with the heavenly so his modal jarring music creates space for evil; however, the fact that he outlives Teague reinforces the positive messages of the story.

Both male parents are widowed and are lone figures in the novel. The pattern then follows that both daughters survive, have children and go on to weave together their own respective cultural messages, mountain wisdom, Cherokee and 'received' educated values into a much stronger resource.

SECONDARY CHARACTERS

As some characters appear to be constructed around one or two traits, they can have a static effect on the narrative. So characters such as Teague, the goat woman and Veasey do not develop in themselves, but their existence ensures that the protagonist Inman does evolve.

CHECK THE NET
For stories and folklore from Cherokee culture visit **www.cherokee byblood.com**

VEASEY

Veasey travels with Inman for several chapters and encounters danger with him. However, he enters the novel as a scoundrel, and proves to be unreliable and selfish, in contrast to Inman's stronger morality. Veasey has been educated in biblical lore; he is mentally acute and uses his intelligence to describe Inman and justify his actions. He is a comic character, with his pretensions and reckless idiocy, yet he is a mouthpiece for another more pragmatic philosophy about survival and pleasure that Inman must take into account. Veasey's own wanderings include punishment and death. His character does not develop as such, but perhaps he represents some of the choices Inman might have made, had he less self-control.

TEAGUE

The other character who repeatedly enters the narrative is Teague, who acts as the persecutor figure throughout. Portrayed as a remarkable man, clearly skilled in mountain survival, listening to messages from nature, he is coolly savage as he kills ordinary farmers and anyone who is harbouring outliers. He is depicted indirectly more than once through others' stories, and this creates layers of threat as he gradually looms into view, before coming into direct conflict with first Stobrod and Pangle, and then finally Inman himself, on the mountain. He functions as an inevitable threat in the narrative; his death coincides with the end of this threat to Ada and Ruby.

PANGLE

Pangle belongs to the world of music and mountain. He lives on the mountain more comfortably than any other character; he is simple and expects little from others, but somehow 'belongs' to Stobrod from the moment he hears his fiddle music. Pangle allows Stobrod's nurturing side to come out, so that we see the latter as worthy of a second chance. Ruby sees him as a fellow outsider, which suggests that he and she have plenty in common. He cannot lie or obscure the truth, which is his downfall as he naively tells Teague where the outliers' cave is. There is great pathos to be drawn from his character, particularly at his death.

QUESTION

How is villainy presented in the novel? Do you feel Teague is alone in representing malign influences?

THEMES

JOURNEYS AND PILGRIMAGE

The principal framework of the novel is Inman's physical journey; at one point he thinks: 'this journey will be the axle of my life' (Chapter 3, p. 67). With frequent references to sin and the search for wholeness, the story insists on pilgrimage as a key theme. However, it is worth registering the slight distinction between an odyssey, which has the flavour of a personal, spiritual as well as physical voyage; and a pilgrimage, an arduous journey undertaken to atone for a sinful or flawed state of mind. Both apply to Inman; clearly he is escaping his enemy (Federal and Confederate soldiers and the Home Guard), and also seeking to cure his disordered thoughts.

Religious pilgrimage figures widely in early Western literature; and external expiation of sin for internal chaos or error is a rich metaphoric plot line, used, of course, in Geoffrey Chaucer's *Canterbury Tales*, in William Langland's *Piers Plowman*, in stories of the Gawain poet from the Middle Ages as well as *Everyman*, and John Bunyan's seventeenth-century work *The Pilgrim's Progress*. Pilgrimages were undertaken to atone for sins committed against the heavenly order, but also came to be, as in *The Canterbury Tales*, a social gathering of all classes, backgrounds and human types, with religious and moral health as the 'levelling' aspiration for all.

In Dante's *Divine Comedy* too, the male protagonist must descend through various versions of hell and purgatory before he re-emerges to health and wholeness. The religious imagery of these works has greatly influenced much of Western literature; here in *Cold Mountain* it gains a new relevance with allusions to the Civil War's chaos and destruction as a kind of hell on earth. And American literature, strongly coloured by puritan ideals, makes particular use of ideas of men working their way through the wilderness and up to the 'city on the hill'; this has helpful parallels with Inman fighting his way away from war and back to the higher ground of his own moral mountain.

Other examples are the 'foul place called Happy Valley' (Chapter 11, p. 250); and the 'miry slough' of 'brown flatland' (Chapter 3, p. 65) which is strongly symbolic of the state of Inman's mind. He is

 CHECK THE BOOK

In his 1942 book *On Native Grounds: An Interpretation of Modern American Prose Literature*, Alfred Kazin examines what he calls 'the shadowy tragic strain in modern American writing'.

portrayed as a 'dark monk out awander for the good of his soul' (Chapter 13, p. 290); more than once he is trapped in fog, goes in circles, or loses his way. Inman's various comforters and helpers as he travels might be seen to represent attitudes or states of mind, also seen in Christian **allegorical** works.

The novel includes Odell's search for his lover, Veasey's travelling with Inman, the goat woman's wanderings, Stobrod's peripatetic ramblings in and out of communities, as well as Ada's internal changes. Inman himself is pictured as 'a night traveler, a fugitive, an outlier' (Chapter 3, p. 67). He remembers Swimmer's spell: 'Your path lies toward the Nightland. This is your path. There is no other' (Chapter 3, p. 72). At the end of the novel Inman is again lucid about his position: 'A wandering pilgrim in my own place' (Chapter 18, p. 391).

To find direction Inman often uses the heavens, the Milky Way and the 'sky for orientation' (Chapter 9, p. 221); again the allegory of the journey represents spiritual enlightenment and ethical choices made. He has an internal 'dark voice' which threatens him with bitterness and anger, with 'No map nor guidebook for such journey' (Chapter 18, p. 384). Native American culture is also invoked by Frazier when he uses the Shining Rocks of the Cherokee **myth**; Inman tells Ada the story before he leaves (Chapter 10, pp. 240–2), and later he tinkers with the idea of death, wondering whether he should 'keep on going into that happy valley' (Chapter 18, p. 380). Here travelling towards oblivion is suggested as a remedy to the ills of his psyche.

In the first chapter Inman counsels his enemies, the Federals, to 'Go home' (p. 11), and this search for homeland, 'His place', is wrought in many forms in the story. He wonders if he must always 'wander singular' (Chapter 9, p. 222), and Ada too must find her bearings; on Cold Mountain in the final chapters she realises that 'No direction could be ruled out' (Chapter 17, p. 375), and that she is looking for a 'set of points that no longer existed' (Chapter 17, p. 364). Ada's grasp of the metaphor of journeying helps her recognise Stobrod's music as redemptive in Chapter 12 (p. 286).

CHECK THE NET

A strong tradition of songs and folk music was a feature of the time; in Chapter 10 Ada buys some sheet music by Stephen Foster (1826–64), who wrote 'Oh! Susanna' (1848). Find further information on contemporary music of the American Civil War at **www. civilwarmusic.net**

ROMANTIC LOVE

There are various versions of passionate or romantic love between men and women in *Cold Mountain*. Inman rarely talks directly of love for Ada but one instance is in conversation with the goat woman, which is somewhat obliquely delivered: 'the verdict he had come to at the hospital was that he loved her' (Chapter 11, p. 268). Inman's journey home is, however, fuelled principally by the desire to see Ada, to experience some peace and a future with her.

Early in the novel Inman's fascination with Ada is represented in standard terms of physical attraction: 'all he wanted was to place two fingertips against that mystery place' (Chapter 3, p. 74), and this developed into a chance meeting in Monroe's kitchen, where she 'rested in his lap' (Chapter 4, p. 97). Their farewell was partly bungled as Inman went off to war, yet the narrative constantly reminds us of Inman's need for Ada and the comfort she brings him through his journey.

Inman's understated feelings as he travels keep the element of growing fondness for an idealised Ada pulsing away in the reader's mind: 'The vision of Ada would not loose its grip on his mind, nor did he wish it to' (Chapter 5, p. 127). Yet there had been scant contact between the two, even before Inman left. This would of course accord with the era in which they lived, as well as the general sense of separation undergone by many characters in the book.

Inman's lack of physical contact from any female is exposed in Sara's cabin: 'A woman had not touched a hand to him with any degree of tenderness in so long' (Chapter 13, p. 299). A clear line can be drawn between this lowest time and later in the Cherokee village when Ada also touches Inman's torso, feeling for his weight loss; in his vagrant and desperate state, her tenderness is overwhelming for him. Love as a great potential force is communicated to the reader through Inman's feelings, arguably more so than through Ada's. When he sees her in the clearing, dressed like a man, he feels 'overcome by love like a ringing in his soul' (Chapter 18, p. 391). But the idealised version is tempered by humorous reality too, as when Ada undresses and has to 'crow-hop twice' in her man's britches (Chapter 19, p. 416).

CHECK THE BOOK

For some insights into American romanticism and pastoral ideals read Lawrence Buell's essay 'American Literary Emergence as a Postcolonial Phenomenon' in *American Literature, American Culture*, edited by Gordon Hutner (1998).

ROMANTIC LOVE continued

CHECK THE FILM

Anthony Minghella's 2003 film portrays Ada as more of a Southern belle than an educated woman. What sorts of tensions might Ada's education and schooling in Western cultural ways set up in the novel?

It is also worth noting that when the lovers come together before Inman dies, it takes place in a mysterious setting, where others have lived brief desperate lives and where Ada senses loss, 'so total and so soon' (p. 375). Their love is overshadowed by dark elements such as this, in spite of their hopeful future planning. In fact, 'normal' paired interaction in a stable domestic setting is **ironically** confined to the Sara and Inman encounter.

Turning to Ada, Frazier depicts much of her early prickly nature through her attitude to love and marriage; she has no intention of marrying and delivers this edict to her peers in Charleston: 'Marriage is the end of woman' (Chapter 2, p. 61). Brusque and chilly to Inman at their first meeting, her gradual recognition of her feelings for him, culminating in her letter ('Come back to me is my request'), and the realisation that 'saying what your heart felt, straight and simple' is what is most important (Chapter 14, pp. 331–2) are distinct milestones in her inner journey to self-knowledge.

There is also an absence of love between men and women in the novel: listening to Ruby's story of the heron raping her mother is shocking for Ada and the reader; yet as an antidote to this, in the same chapter Ada recounts her own parents' finally realised love. Odell's story includes an order from his father that he should just use the slave girl, and not commit to her. Ultimately, on their first night together, Ada and Inman are 'woven together on their bed of hemlock boughs' (Chapter 19, p. 417), which **foreshadows** Ada's retelling of the Baucis and Philemon **myth** in the epilogue (p. 435). Here the love between the mythical pair seems to be a fitting culmination of the story of Inman and Ada, and their misfortune is in some senses 'healed' by this myth of cleaving together and wholeness.

Romance and passion surface through other characters too: we see it in Odell and the slave his father owns: 'looking down at her pretty little feet he wished his wife was dead' (Chapter 7, p. 163); the goat woman and the boy she kisses on the way home; and in Sara's grief for her dead husband. To balance the tragic and sombre versions of wasted love in the novel is Ruby's characteristic reaction to attraction, delineated in predictably comic terms as she gives Reid a 'foot in the back … a hug otherwise' (Epilogue, p. 433). Veasey also is not let off scot-free by Inman for his unwise lack of self-control with Laura: 'your britches around your ankles' (Chapter 5, p. 113) is our lasting image of their relationship.

War and ruined romance are forcefully linked in the novel; the wretched and irrecoverable losses in battle are somehow all the more desperate because of love affairs as well as lives foreshortened. Grieving wounded soldiers on battlefields are given solace through romantic music, with the strains of 'Cora Ellen' and 'Lorena' drifting across the bodies at Fredericksburg (Chapter 1, pp. 10–11). In contrast to this is Sara's 'squeal of barren lonesomeness' as she sings '*bride bed full of blood*', an unsettling murder ballad which adds a layer of hopelessness to the perspectives on marriage in the novel (Chapter 13, p. 310).

On the theme of idealised love, Ada's contemporaries in Charleston suddenly acquire gallant and heroic charms, and 'wished' they 'might become somebody's darling' (Chapter 6, p. 135). Blount's tears as he rowed out on the lake with Ada are all the more ironic and affecting for the reader due to our heightened awareness of loss to come, particularly of such young men in the first flush of youth and possible romance. Sometimes romantic love creates quiet and settled moments in an otherwise frenetic and hazardous narrative: the story pauses briefly in these one-on-one interactions, as, for example, when Ada and Inman walked together and took shelter under a coat to talk.

ORDER AND CHAOS

The novel contains many references to patterns and disorder; each of Inman's stopping points is suggestive of either ordered meaning or its antithesis, chaos.

The goat woman and the gypsy camp contain various harmonious ways of living. In contrast is Junior's farm, where children trace random patterns on the floor and have little power of speech; or the war itself, where the soldiers are like 'a pen of shoats' (Chapter 7, p. 153). Inman himself searches for patterns, if not in coffee grounds as in the first chapter, then in behaviour: 'I do not understand you people' (Chapter 9, p. 216). He wishes

> **CONTEXT**
>
> Written by the Reverend H. D. L. Webster in 1856, 'Lorena' was a very popular song among Confederate soldiers. It was about yearning for a sweetheart and longing for home.

QUESTION

The chaos of war seems to aggravate underlying misunderstandings in the community. How crucial is cultural harmony to the novel?

not to be 'smirched with the mess of other people' (Chapter 5, p. 119).

Remaining intellectually lucid is essential for Inman, as we see at Junior's farm, where he is drugged. 'His thoughts would not serve his purpose. They refused to achieve order or proportion' (Chapter 9, p. 212), and he is thereby caught by the Home Guard, his main enemy. After the prisoners are shot, Inman wakes up as if from the dead, and sees 'a smattering of light cast patternless on the general dark' (Chapter 9, p. 220). Via the helping agency of the slave and the goat woman he regains a sense of geographical and moral order and is reoriented towards his goal, Cold Mountain.

In Ada's story the farm at Black Cove is in disarray and Ada requires Ruby's help to reorder it. Ruby knows intimately how to work with the shapes and forms of nature and is closely connected to survival. Ada learns how to manage the land, accepting Ruby's belief in natural **portents** as 'concern for the patterns and tendencies of the material world' (Chapter 6, p. 129). Inman craves contact with these patterns of normal life but fears he is 'deeply at variance with such elements of the harmonious' (Chapter 11, p. 266).

Veasey's account of God's moral order is shaky: 'Note especially the way He uses fire and flood. Have you ever seen a pattern of justice in their application?' (Chapter 9, p. 195); and part of Stobrod's influence through his music is to 'give order and meaning to a day's end' (Chapter 12, p. 284).

Ada searches for meaning too: Monroe and her education have taught her to do this via intellect and metaphors, but she alters her view to find that 'Whatever a book said would lack something essential' (Chapter 17, p. 364).

FATE

There are numerous references to a force that seems to hover over the characters in the novel. At times benign and akin to guardianship, at others it is depicted as a malevolent force: 'a dark-fisted hand' (Chapter 8, p. 184) or, more generally, 'all the world hanging over ... ready to drop and crush' (Chapter 13, p. 294). At times these elements give the novel a strong flavour of fatalism as the small men or women appear to be just playthings of a higher force. As in many classical **myths**, and specifically in Homer's *Odyssey*, the gods play with mortals and place them in impossible situations; Frazier's craft here echoes this technique as he ensures that Inman feels like 'the butt of the celestial realm' (Chapter 3, p. 67). And more broadly, human ambition and expectation are repeatedly undercut in the novel, as when Inman sees a picture in the goat woman's caravan with the inscription: 'Our personal lives are brief indeed' (Chapter 11, p. 258).

A similar technique is used in **naturalistic** genre novels, where characters are seen more as functions of their environment than as fully independent beings. For example, when Inman is roped to the band of outliers, the men appear as faceless victims who will not be remembered after their deaths: 'without hardly making any mark more lasting than plowing a furrow' (Chapter 9, p. 216).

On the other hand, the novel contains historically verifiable details, particularly in its early chapters. These facts have the effect of 'levelling' the narrative in favour of actualities and events. Likewise the final settled chapter depicts humans in charge of the order; any pernicious external influences have been expunged and harmony reigns.

THE PLACE OF PEOPLE IN NATURE

The mountain at the heart of the novel takes several shapes, and is at times threatening, at others nurturing. Nature is a force to reckon with; the goat woman says there is 'a world of food growing volunteer if you know where to look' (Chapter 11, p. 262). Even Teague with his savage nature seems to listen out for messages which tell him how to behave. Ruby, the goat woman and Pangle seem to be most in touch with the force of nature; Ada and Inman are 'taught' by them how to recast their moral values. Inman recognises 'His place' both physically and morally as he regains the foothills near home (Chapter 15, p. 343).

Monroe chose this landscape to live in, seeing in it 'some other world, some deeper life with a whole other existence' (Chapter 6, p. 139). Frazier underlines the shaky place of humanity in the world in the epigraph where he quotes Darwin: 'the … quiet war of

WWW. CHECK THE NET

The various American Civil War battles, many of them close to the area through which Inman travels, are explained in some detail at **www. americancivilwar. com**. The website includes in particular a helpful timeline of the battles mentioned in the novel.

CONTEXT

There are two epigraphs in *Cold Mountain*: one from Darwin, one from a poem by Han-shan. Han-shan was a Chinese poet and hermit in the eighth or ninth century; his name translated into English is Cold Mountain.

organic beings, going on in the peaceful woods, & smiling fields' – and in one sense the novel might be said to debate this very issue.

Ada is the character who learns the most about nature and where she fits into it. When Ruby asks her: 'What do you hear?', Ada's response makes her retort contemptuously: 'Trees ... Just general trees is all? You've got a long way to go' (Chapter 12, pp. 277–8). Not long after, Ada decides to answer the question 'Where am I?' with 'You are here, in this one station, now' (Chapter 14, p. 318). Her musings on the farm, the sky and the seasons have taught her to narrow her compass of enquiry to her immediate environment.

Taught by nature when still a child, Ruby, like Pangle, belongs to it. The earth is 'a guardian that took her under its wing and concerned itself with her well-being' (Chapter 4, p. 103). Nature is entirely benevolent in the final scenes of the book: crows and trees are part of Inman's heavenly vision; the harvest has provided well for Ada's family in the epilogue. But as the search on the mountain shows, with the fog, the twisted and forked paths, nature is not always helpful or wholesome. The metaphors of isolation in the novel rely heavily on nature, on figures like isolated herons or lone ducks and crows, or the herb goldenseal that heals human wounds. Inman is seen taking shelter in bird houses and trees. But when Stobrod and Pangle are shot, the great poplar tree remains upright, if slightly scarred.

NARRATIVE TECHNIQUES

STRUCTURE

The two main linear narratives are the framework for the novel; in twenty chapters and an epilogue the travelling of Inman and the waiting of Ada serve as the key thrusts towards a goal. Interwoven are stories of others which, although halting the narrative progress towards the reunion of the lovers, in fact add depth and vigorous colour to the general sense of existence in the fraught months at the end of the Civil War. Hearing of Odell's failed love affair or the goat woman's lost sweetheart is as instructive for Inman as Ada's learning of Ruby's childhood pains and tribulations and her father's long-lasting passion for her mother.

Cold Mountain is a highly metaphorical novel (as discussed in **Imagery and symbolism**). Examples of recurring metaphors are crows, pilgrims, stars and weather. The numerous natural allusions tie the narrative to a seemingly omnipotent universal force, which alongside the geographical place names add a degree of solidity to the story. The seasons and the jobs they entail, the ways the mountain changes, 'a mottle of color rising behind the house' (Epilogue, p. 434), also act as organising factors in the characters' lives.

Teague and his influence reappear, as befits a villain, at key moments to re-engage the reader in the latent peril of Inman's journey. Comfort and order are swapped for pain and chaos, and then swing back to relative peace.

Frazier contracts time at some points; days of wandering for Inman or farm work for Ada and Ruby receive general description but nothing more. The desire to return home is the main momentum for Inman, and as he approaches Cold Mountain, the sense of arriving replaces his lost moral state.

Tangential narratives enhance the linear path of the novel. Along with named characters such as Veasey and Odell, Inman meets slaves, starving and crazy people. Parallel to this broader perspective is Ada's gradual familiarity with her own closely observed world, knowing which trees sound in which ways, how to split certain kinds of wood and suchlike, the 'luminous quiver' (Chapter 6, p. 134) of insect life. Thus the two thrusts, one broader and one specific, keep the reader focused on the concept of 'home' and safety.

Flashbacks (or **analepses**) ensure that we know details of Monroe, Inman's boyhood, Ruby's and Ada's parentage; and the effect is to substantiate the main characters' dilemmas and choices. For example it is key that we understand Stobrod's abandonment of Ruby to comprehend her later cynicism.

NARRATORS AND POINTS OF VIEW

Cold Mountain contains various stories of survival and these strands of narrative offer a variety of perspectives. The former lives of Odell, the outlier in jail, and Ruby and Stobrod are narrated by an

CHECK THE FILM

Anthony Minghella's 2003 film copies the parallel narratives of the novel, and occasionally develops further stories, such as Stobrod's playing his fiddle for an Appalachian soldier's passing, or the invention of the murder of the Swanger sons by Teague's Home Guard. This overlapping of stories acts as an extra thrust in the film, culminating in a meeting of paths at the end.

QUESTION

What effects do the various voices and speakers in the novel have on our sense of perspective?

external third-person narrator, yet it is clearly shown that these accounts 'belong' to the characters. This narrator 'understands' the feelings of the characters, and has the effect of being 'internal', and is thus what we might call omniscient. However, although he or she presents the consciousness from within, the narrator does not pass judgement and is not intrusive.

This **omniscient narrator** orders and orchestrates the various speakers, either to offer prominence or to withdraw at key points. An example is where Ruby and her father retell a moment in their lives from their own respective points of view. Here Frazier allows Ruby to tell her story directly: 'You came and went and I could have been there or not when you got back' (Chapter 14, p. 328). Yet Stobrod's version is told via the third person: 'He and a partner had taken the notion of making liquor for profit …' (Chapter 14, p. 329). Frazier adds tone and style from Stobrod to the facts of his story. On the other hand, Monroe retells the account of his marriage via the first person, his tone directly presented as he recounts his version of reality to Ada: 'It is a thing that keeps coming into my mind of late' (Chapter 8, p. 189).

Occasionally the narrator is heard over the action, as when Inman has to choose whether or not to kill the bear cub. 'To his credit', we are told, he does consider letting it live (Chapter 15, p. 341), but finally does 'all he could do' (p. 342).

However, the novel deals most specifically with two stories: those of Inman and Ada. Inman's battle experiences are told with him firmly at the centre: 'Inman's only thought looking on the enemy was, Go home' (Chapter 1, p. 11), but surrounded by historically recorded details: 'a vast army marching uphill toward a stone wall' (p. 7), which creates an effect of verisimilitude by anchoring the narrative to recorded facts. The former quotation is evidence of Frazier's skill as a narrator: he embeds Inman's emotions about the war in a two-word phrase which offers us key information about Inman. The 'vast army' phrase also offers the account some sense of history, which lends the text factual solidity.

Different points of view are sometimes directly flagged up, as when Ruby and Ada react differently to the outlier's tale. The technique of third-person narration might be said to distance us from their emotions. Inman and Ada have differing versions of the same memory of Monroe's Christmas party. The slight **dissonance** between their two stories adds colour and individual depth to our sense of them as discrete characters.

The use of **analepsis** filtered through characters' memory appears to contradict the linear shape of the story – for example the reader knows that Monroe is dead long before we see him die or see how Ada coped with his death. Revisiting the scene fleshes out her motivations and current **persona** in the action. So although the text goes through a time shift, the reader synthesises it into a general picture

Narrative is in fact a key issue in the story, as well as the vehicle which carries the story. Inman wants to hear of the goat woman's life; Veasey too is curious about Inman's life; and Ruby and Ada escape their current state when they listen to and tell stories in the evenings. Inman also decides shortly before he dies that he will not reveal much of his story: 'you could tell such things on and on and yet no more get to the full truth of the war' (Chapter 19, p. 418); and both Ada and he retell their childhoods as if they were 'idylls' (Chapter 19, p. 417).

The broad sweep of *Cold Mountain* means that other narratives seem to jostle for space in the novel: accounts from the Cherokee culture and the Trail of Tears, presented via Swimmer and his spells and Inman hearing the Shining Rocks story; the gypsy band's memories of their travels; the outlier's tales; Mrs McKennet's romanticised war story; Sara's sad tale of loss; and so on.

LANGUAGE AND STYLE

Perhaps the most prominent linguistic feature of the novel is its use of a specific **vernacular** and old speech rhythms. Ruby, Stobrod, Inman and many other lesser characters have strong dialects, an effect that features in many **realist** genre novels by authors such as Thomas Hardy and Charles Dickens. An example would be the

? QUESTION

Clay Reynolds, a fellow novelist, has written of *Cold Mountain*: 'One feels the weariness of the characters, their hunger and their misery, just as one experiences the depths of their emotions, the extremes of their desperation.' Do you feel any characters are more effectively drawn than others?

slave who feeds Inman before he kills Junior: 'They Lord God amighty, he said. You look like a dirt man' (Chapter 9, p. 222). Some commentators have judged the **archaisms** as designed to distance the reader from the narrator, to flag up the work as somehow historically authentic. Read out loud the text assumes a kind of rhythm; **syntax** and pace are measured and have some **epic**, even biblical, undertones, which echo the *Odyssey* and stories of the wandering of Christ in the desert. And 'then he left that place behind him' (Chapter 13, p. 307) is typical of this technique with its sententious and scriptural tone.

Where Frazier's use of this technique diverges slightly from the realist genre is in the narrator's own contribution, often delivered in syntactically unusual structures, and with some archaic vocabulary choices. Again when Inman is fed by the slave, the narrator elucidates his feelings: 'The invisible world, he declared to himself, had abandoned him as a gypsy soul to wander singular, without guide or chart, through a broken world composed of little but impediment' (Chapter 9, p. 222).

Dialogue itself is often rendered in a synthesised, abbreviated format, as in Ruby's reunion with her father:

— So you're not dead? Ruby said.

— Not yet, said Stobrod. Set your daddy loose.

(Chapter 12, p. 274)

Here the characters' interactions, internal reactions and utterances speed up action, reveal relationships and create mystery.

Ada and her father, on the other hand, speak using educated diction and register, as does Veasey, though his language is laced with biblical reference, which adds its own colour. The frequent mention of metaphor and interpretation by Ada and Monroe suggests that language itself is an indicator of their character and thematic development. Ada must learn to substitute for her habitual dense figurative enquiry a simpler angle on life. Inman is recognisably less eloquent than she is but makes pithy comments in relation to all situations, as with Veasey's dubious moral standards:

'It is still a cloudy matter to me if I did the right thing, letting you live' (Chapter 7, p. 145).

Part of the style of the book is its discriminating and sage tone: the narrator follows Inman on his journeys and uses an ethical angle on his choice to lie with Sara: 'It was his lot to bear the penalty of the unredeemed, that tenderness be forevermore denied him and that his life be marked down a dark mistake' (Chapter 13, p. 299).

There is also a prosaic rhythm that can be frequently seen in some of the more dense natural descriptions of the novel.

IMAGERY AND SYMBOLISM

The symbolic language of *Cold Mountain* operates on a number of levels; there are repeated references to crows, herons, other birds, the stars, the moon, water and paths, all of which belong to the lexis of moral wandering and orientation within nature. In the first pages of the novel Inman feels he is 'lonesome and estranged from all around him as a sad old heron standing pointless watch' (Chapter 1, p. 20). Some characters too are **motifs** of states of mind or particular choices, such as the goat woman and her hermit-like world, or Veasey and his lustful ways. Inman is tempted by both these worlds, either to seek oblivion and die (or hide) or to follow his carnal desires.

The goat woman in particular appears at a pivotal point of Inman's journey: her role is to heal him (and hear of his worst fears and dearest desires) but then she is left behind, as if she belongs only to a stage of his learning process. **Epic** and moral works, such as the *Odyssey* and *Everyman* respectively, make use of these rather 'monotone' symbolic representations, even directly linking characters' natures to their names, a device which has strong links with the literary technique of **allegory**.

Ada is accustomed to the language of symbolism on account of her education and life with Monroe; her life with Ruby adds a more tangible link between states of mind and the world around her. Frazier depicts her new symbols and motifs with vigour and energy (Epilogue, p. 434).

> **CONTEXT**
>
> Rebirth is a potent metaphor in literature and religion alike. Inman, like Odysseus, must die to others or himself in order to regain a foothold on his own scale of values.

CHECK THE FILM

Consider the ways in which Anthony Minghella uses mysticism in his 2003 film *Cold Mountain*, for example with the horses on the battlefield in the opening shots. How do these mirror the mystical elements in the novel?

Nature and its various faces have heavy symbolic weight in the novel, none less than the goal of the mountain, which begins to assume biblical proportions as Inman nears the foothills and even goes by Moravian and Quaker farms for safety and food.

PART FOUR

CRITICAL HISTORY

RECEPTION AND EARLY REVIEWS

Cold Mountain was lavishly praised as soon as it was published in 1997, by fellow writers as well as by critics. Alfred Kazin in the *New York Times Book Review* described Frazier's prose as 'silky and arch in capturing the stiff speech of the period'. The novelist Claire Messud, writing in the *Washington Post Book World*, made particular reference to the 'antiquated style' and the vocabulary which 'thrills in its oddity'. In addition, the detailed historical context, the breadth of reference and the economy of the plot line elicited almost universal respect.

Rick Bass, also a novelist, has enthused and talked about *Cold Mountain* in classic terms: 'The shadow of this book and the joy I received in reading it will fall over every other book I ever read ... one of the great accomplishments of American literature'. *Cold Mountain* won the National Book Award, and its great success among the critics was echoed in the response of the public too.

Some critics have concentrated on its historical features in order to explain its attraction for the modern reader. Although Frazier's novel clearly uses history for the backdrop to the love story of Inman and Ada, the degree to which it does so might be an issue given that the central thrust of the book is the love affair between the hero and heroine, conceivably a 'timeless' plot. Kevin Grauke (2002), on the other hand, focuses on the relevance of *Cold Mountain* for modern Americans, stating that 'How we tell the story of the Civil War structures the cultural narrative of the United States'.

Barry Lopez in a 1997 essay entitled 'A Literature of Place' explained that writing 'that takes into account the impact nature and place have on culture is one of the oldest – and perhaps most singular – threads in American writing'. Frazier clearly joins this tradition with *Cold Mountain*, particularly as he explores the

CHECK THE BOOK

Kevin Grauke's article 'Vietnam, Survivalism and the Civil War: The Use of History in Michael Shaara's *The Killer Angels* and Charles Frazier's *Cold Mountain*' (*WLA*, 2002) considers the landscape of Inman's journey as 'nearly post-apocalyptic in its bleakness'. Grauke goes on to describe the epilogue as a picture of a 'self-sufficient sphere' where the characters are isolated and 'oblivious to the struggles' of post-war reconstruction.

spiritual values of the North Carolina mountains, and their remedies for the carnage of war. Early in the novel Inman feels a loathing for the 'metal face of the age' (Chapter 1, p. 2); his task is to determine the correct and least destructive road to his own atonement for his part in this war, something also identified in Lopez's essay: Inman must 'distinguish between roads to heaven and detours to hell'.

CONTEMPORARY APPROACHES

Due to the fact that *Cold Mountain* was published in the late twentieth century, much has yet to be written on the text from a critical perspective. Nevertheless, several strands of contemporary criticism have relevance for the study of the novel and should be of use to students when considering the text from a critical angle.

FEMINISM

CHECK THE BOOK
A helpful introduction to Marxism, post-colonialism and feminism can be found in Peter Barry's *Beginning Theory: An Introduction to Literary and Cultural Theory* (1995).

Feminist approaches in literature cover a wide field of enquiry, including how women write about themselves, how they are represented in literature, and how the language used about and by them matches reality. The questions that might be worth asking in regard to a feminist approach are therefore: how does the picture of Ada, Ruby, Sally Swanger, Mrs McKennet, Sara, Tildy, Laura and so on, accord with the reality of women's lives, and more precisely the reality of American life in the 1860s? Are they constructed as 'gendered' figures in the novel, and if so how? And on another level, is our reading of their lives and experiences coloured by our own gendered responses?

A feminist position might be that Inman's journey is a linear trajectory and therefore belongs to patriarchal discourse, whereas Ada's new world view is confidently cyclical, paying attention to seasons, stars and weather, and therefore more relevant to female experience. In the Cherokee village, Inman enters a female-run world: the women are dressed as men, they shoot game, haul in wood, make all the decisions. As at Sara's cabin, he must play by the women's rules.

Equally some critics might take the view that Inman has passed through a world of male values, beaten it and transformed himself back into the natural world man he was prior to the war. He and Ada can now meet on new territory with Ada running a productive farm, able to survive; and Inman having cast off some of the **persona** of a soldier. Many times on his travels he receives female help.

Ruby becomes Ada's 'text' (Chapter 6, p. 132), which could be evidence of her power to challenge rationalist and masculine philosophy, especially obvious in the references to Emerson. Ada has to rethink her philosophical lessons, taught her by her father (and without a mother's care to balance her outlook), and re-emerge as a woman with self-respect and the ability to use and view the world around her in a 'female' way.

Some feminist analysis focuses on the level of language and self-expression available to women to express the reality around them: when she arrives from Charleston, Ada is gauche and detached from her new reality as well as her previous one. The female world of the parlour at Monroe's Christmas party was uncomfortable for her, with its talk of 'one baby after another' and 'little more than wiping tails' (Chapter 4, p. 95). She has also rebuffed the standard female path of marriage, and could not utter false comfort to Blount on the lake.

Charles Frazier's language, with its attention to finding one's own metaphors and the ways it seems to seek and alter received meanings, could be construed as pro-female. Frazier devotes a lot of attention to Ada finding her place and a code that explains her view of life, which for some feminist critics is the sine qua non of literary discourse. French feminists such as Hélène Cixous look for female writing which eschews all forms of masculine discourse.

Many women in the novel are powerless. A feminist critic might consider what has led to their state and how the story ultimately ascribes power or lack of it. Ruby's early life is motherless, at the whim of a careless man, but she learns how to survive by watching other women; and later she recreates her family with her in the driving seat over her father. She also passes the female kinship skills on to Ada, and Ada then brings up her own daughter using this template.

CHECK THE BOOK

Marcus Cunliffe's *The Literature of the United States* (1954) has a chapter entitled 'Women's Voices', which is a good starting point for research on American women writing in the nineteenth century.

CONTEXT

The work of Hélène Cixous (1937–) is mainly concerned with the relationship between psychoanalysis and language, particularly in its significance for women, as well as examining the links between the reader and the writer.

A feminist critic might examine the 'otherness' of the women in *Cold Mountain*. This has links to post-colonial criticism covered below, but for feminist critical theory, it centres on how the until recently accepted canon of literature has insisted on male experience and values to be the substantial stories and narratives of human existence. For example, **epic** literature such as the *Odyssey* follows male protagonists on their adventures and moral journeys. By association, women are also seen as extraneous to the main narrative thrust. However, in *Cold Mountain* it is fairly straightforward to see that the narrative is equally balanced in terms of gendered accounts.

The outcome of the main female characters' lives, as mothers of their families, might be judged a positive enforcement of the female world over the destruction of the warring years.

MARXISM

Marxist criticism examines how class and ideology affect literary works. Social and economic context is the key factor in that it informs the ideas and concerns of the writer, and, secondarily, those of the reader too. Some Marxist critics might state of *Cold Mountain* that it validates the existing social structure (although it contains implicit and explicit criticism of the world itself) by using the form of the **realist** novel with a chronological time scheme and in-depth characterisation, a standard beginning and ending.

A Marxist critic might focus on the rational issues of economic production in the novel: for example Ruby knows how to produce food from raw materials; she is an efficient means of production; she can barter and distribute according to her needs. Ada belongs more to the superstructure, a cultured world of art, philosophy and ideas. Inman is coming from a ravaged world where the class struggles of American history are being resolved through war.

There are suffering and disenfranchised people throughout Inman's wanderings; they too are the result, in a Marxist critic's eyes, of a nation state making the change from feudalism to a modern industrial economy. The Federal soldiers are victims of this depersonalised system as much as the slaves are on Odell's father's estate.

CONTEXT

In Marxist theory, the superstructure refers to the culture and institutions believed to reflect or result from the economic system underlying a society.

For a Marxist critic, class is more significant then personality. Using this model, Ada's class is reconfigured. Her early condescension would be, in a Marxist critic's eyes, evidence of her privileged world and language. Ruby's rejection of her airs and graces undercuts Ada's power, and establishes in its place a materialist world view.

Inman and Ada too are from different social layers: she from the wealthy and cultured South, he from an impoverished mountain village. He belongs to the world which produces; she belongs to the world of consumption, with her hat which has travelled halfway round the world. The narrative pulls their opposite factors into relationship, largely through the intervention of war and social strife. A Marxist critic would recognise this scenario as part of inevitable social progression.

POST-COLONIAL READINGS

The concepts of post-colonial theory entered the study of literature in the late 1970s and early 1980s. This school of thought focuses on issues of 'difference' in a text and rejects ideas of norms in Western texts as literary standards. It therefore discards any concept of the Western tradition as an overarching literary benchmark. It does not accept the canon (which became generally accepted as a valid marker of quality in literature with the publication of F. R. Leavis's *The Great Tradition* in 1948) as the standard by which other forms of literature are judged. On the contrary, the post-colonial movement values and celebrates 'otherness'.

Cold Mountain could be viewed from this post-colonial perspective, given that the narrative includes racial and other social divides, along with the abuse of power over whole ethnic groups. It could also be said that the novel, along with all American literature since the Declaration of Independence in 1776, might use a voice which is in itself post-colonial, since it arises from history that also has the overthrow of imperial norms at its heart – in this case European, principally British, norms. Another issue is that there are ambiguities in an approach to mainstream American writing being viewed in a post-colonial light, given that the United States is the only real superpower on the planet. Lawrence Buell in his article 'American Literary Emergence as a Postcolonial Phenomenon' in *American Literature, American Culture*, edited by Gordon Hutner

www. CHECK THE NET

In her article 'True Stories', published in the *Guardian* on 16 June 2000, Ros Coward explores the 'construction of history as narrative' and wonders if we are 'lapping up what we can read about significant moments in the construction of modernity because we sense we are in the middle of another shift in what we know and think'. To read this article in its entirety, go to **http://books.guardian.co.uk** and search for Ros Coward.

(1998), raises questions around the starting point of American post-colonial literature and feelings, and makes reference also to recent 'American imperialism'.

CHECK THE BOOK

All these novels are worth reading in their own right. *The Portrait of a Lady* was written by Henry James and published in 1881; James Fenimore Cooper wrote *The Last of the Mohicans* in 1826 – this gives a vivid picture of Native American and pioneer life. In *The Color Purple* (1982) Alice Walker tells the story of a black woman in the segregated Deep South.

How the protagonist determines his or her identity is a central issue in many American novels such as *The Last of the Mohicans*, *The Portrait of a Lady* and *The Color Purple*; and *Cold Mountain* follows in this tradition. In these works identity, which is 'other' than established received white, male and/or European norms, is at issue. Another position might be that American literature subsumes and later subverts Western literary forms, including satire, polemic, puritan **allegory** and, most interestingly here, the **realist** novel.

To examine writing in terms of the post-colonial theory of 'otherness' is perhaps the more fruitful activity for the purposes of this text. *Cold Mountain* has a plethora of 'others' or outsiders in the story; the novel is peopled with outcasts, whether racially or socially demarcated. The transforming and shifting nature of the journeys gives rise to this factor, and the story itself seeks to discuss issues of equality and cultural meanings, as when Inman hears a discussion about slavery in the gypsy camp. This is a helpful example of the 'other', and in this case 'exotic', characterisation used by Frazier: 'The Ethiopian and the Indians joined in the meal as if they were all of a color and equals' (Chapter 5, p. 123). A post-colonial view might be that this image of the camp shows aliens drawn together almost by virtue of their separation from the status quo, and that they offer a brief ideal of coexisting and cooperating differing cultures to the narrative.

CHECK THE BOOK

If you wish to find out more about the lives and work of many of the authors mentioned in these Notes, *The Oxford Companion to English Literature*, edited by Margaret Drabble, is a good place to begin.

Using the Appalachian **vernacular** might be said by a post-colonial critic to be paying attention to cultural balance. We as readers are forced to recognise a gap between ourselves and the text, and the use of **archaisms** reminds us of differences and otherness in values as well as material distances. Ruby tells the Georgia boy and Ada: 'It was me, I'd about rather rest on the mountain than anywhere else you could name' (Chapter 17, p. 360). Ada too has to learn to measure the relevance of her Western ideals and education against the folkloric patterns she now inhabits.

The slavery issues in the novel take their place alongside studies of rural poverty and the female experience of war. Frazier depicts the misery and outrage of slavery through stories passed on and also through characters delivering judgement on each other. The outlier's tale from the courthouse window includes a scene where his father questioned the ownership of two black Home Guards: 'Their own, I reckon' answered Teague (Chapter 8, p. 177).

Perhaps the most obvious use of otherness in *Cold Mountain* is in the significance ascribed to Cherokee totems and spirits. One view might be that the eclectic range of beliefs and the lack of one defined system of belief in the novel suggest a fragmented world. As Inman walks away from the hospital, knowing that part of his search is for order, he remembers Swimmer's spell: 'Your path lies toward the Nightland. This is your path. There is no other' (Chapter 3, p. 72). Nearing the mountain he stops at a Cherokee rock cairn and places stones on the top, 'as commemoration of some old upward yearning' (Chapter 15, p. 339). His remembering the word 'Cataloochee' and the 'folded landscape' on the mountain (Chapter 15, p. 342) denotes that he is no longer alien, and thus part of his outlier status is nullified. Inman appears to regain his substance as a person by regaining a familiar relationship to his external landscape.

CHECK THE BOOK

For some fascinating and illuminating discussions of the uses of the past in literature, read Edward W. Said's *Culture and Imperialism* (1994), which opens with the statement: 'Appeals to the past are among the commonest of strategies in interpretation of the present'.

PART FIVE

BACKGROUND

CHARLES FRAZIER

Charles Frazier was born in 1950 in Asheville, in the southern area of the Appalachian Mountains. His father was a high-school principal; Frazier attended school and took his undergraduate degree in North Carolina. He carried out further research at the Appalachian State University and then went on to the University of South Carolina for his PhD. *Cold Mountain* is his first novel but he had previously written travel literature and a short story. *Cold Mountain* was published in 1997 and received the National Book Award as well as the Notable Book of the Year Award from the *New York Times*. The film *Cold Mountain*, directed by Anthony Minghella and based on the book, was released in 2003.

WRITING *COLD MOUNTAIN*

Cold Mountain was written over seven years by Charles Frazier, who has spoken of how 'a page a day' was his usual speed of writing. The sources for Frazier's ideas include his childhood memories of family members and the way of life and speech in the Southern Appalachians; a story passed on by his father of an older relative who walked home from the war; and Frazier's own research into journals and diaries of women running farms during wartime. He spent time researching Civil War documents in libraries, which turned up data on the people of the Appalachian communities who got caught in the 'crossfire' of the war which was 'somebody else's battle'.

Frazier has spoken about his sense of writing a book about the return from war rather than the action of fighting itself. It was his resolve to write about 'home and peace', more of an *Odyssey* story than an *Iliad*. Frazier has specifically said of the *Odyssey* that it is a 'literary ancestor' of *Cold Mountain*. It is easy to see how the novel covers a wider picture than a simple war novel might: in *Cold Mountain* war is one element in the life of a community, and passes to reveal a new future for its protagonists.

Frazier has made reference too to his sense of the past, and his

CHECK THE BOOK

Charles Frazier's PhD is entitled *The Geography of Possibility: Man in the Landscape in Recent Western Fiction* (1986).

CHECK THE BOOK

While Homer's *Odyssey* recounts Odysseus's adventures on his journey home from Troy, his *Iliad* describes the war waged against Troy by the Greeks, a siege that lasted ten years.

decision to write *Cold Mountain* in an archaic register as part of his 'elegy' for an 'old America'. Indeed, Frazier's familiarity with the land, its history and culture, moods and seasons, is felt as a strong element throughout the novel.

LITERARY BACKGROUND

Cold Mountain might be said to belong to the genre of war novels, as its principal action is set against the action of war, or those waiting for war to end and loved ones to return home. Many other literary works also fit into this genre, such as *War and Peace* by Leo Tolstoy (published 1865–9), *Birdsong* by Sebastian Faulks (1993), *Regeneration* by Pat Barker (1991), *A Farewell to Arms* by Ernest Hemingway (1929) and *All Quiet on the Western Front* by Erich Maria Remarque (1929). Novels and plays about war are an established and ever developing subgenre. With the advent of Marxist, feminist and post-colonial literary movements (see **Contemporary responses** in **Critical history**), literature about war has become less jingoistic and more inclined to criticise the phenomenon of war. *Cold Mountain* likewise presents an often ambivalent angle on war, showing both sides as victims and aggressors, and takes the overview again that humans hurt each other, some die but their descendants live on.

Epic literature, much of it from Greek and Roman myths, often uses a staple plot line of characters suffering under the yoke of war, or seeking to redress wrongs in battle. Of course the *Odyssey* is firmly within this genre, but so too from a female perspective are plays such as *The Trojan Women* by Euripides, focusing solely on the long wait for loved ones, and the pain it entails. Renaissance dramatists such as William Shakespeare and Christopher Marlowe drew heavily on the theme also. Plays such as *Othello*, *Macbeth*, *Henry V*, *Antony and Cleopatra*, *Julius Caesar* and Marlowe's *Tamburlaine the Great* are crafted around characters who are soldiers, ready to set off to or return from war. And on the female side, Penelope in the *Odyssey*, Desdemona in *Othello* and Lady Macbeth might be said to show interesting similarities to Ada as they attempt to discern and decide their own fates, with or without reference to the men they love.

CHECK THE BOOK

Hemingway's *A Farewell to Arms* tells the story of a love affair between an American soldier and an English nurse during the First World War.

CONTEXT

Euripides (c.480–406) was a Greek tragic playwright. Abandoning painting for literature, he wrote about eighty dramas, of which fewer than twenty survive. *The Trojan Women* was written around 415BC. This play is wholly focused on the experiences of women left behind during the Trojan War, and their sense of betrayal and abandonment by their men, as well as by the gods who decide their fates.

QUESTION

In your view, which characters inject humour and a lighter perspective into the story? How is this achieved?

On a more technical level, *Cold Mountain* belongs most obviously to the **realist** novel genre where the characters are recognisably familiar to us and help to present life 'as it is'. The battle scenes, the cruel deaths on both sides, the social interplay in Charleston and in town when Ruby and Ada visit, depict the respective societies and the choices life presents in each setting. As a result, randomness and oddity, like that of Veasey's behaviour or Teague's savage nature, or even the goat woman's eccentric life, are heightened in effect by their juxtaposition with the prevalent social norms.

There are also hints of the **picaresque** novel, particularly in the wanderings of Veasey and Stobrod, where ridicule and random grandiose ideas inject humour into an otherwise gloomy account. This genre portrays rogues living off their wits in comic circumstances and in a corrupt or disinterested society.

However, the **naturalistic** tendency of the novel, with its detached overview, an almost supervisory godlike force seeming to tinker with characters' fates, establishes another order of precedence in the novel. Thomas Hardy uses this technique repeatedly. His protagonists in, for example, *The Return of the Native* (1878) and *Jude the Obscure* (1895) are tested beyond endurance by a malign external force. As in Renaissance drama such as Shakespeare's *Romeo and Juliet*, the 'script' seems to be already written. Inman's presaging of his probable death, which occurs four times in the narrative, would support this view. More broadly, the 'secret engines of earth' (Epilogue, p. 433) and the tussle between good and evil appear to be the main protagonists of the story at times – human existence may falter, and in war does so on a grand scale, but the future will resume in the end. Human agency in this sense, and realism with it, takes a back seat.

CHECK THE BOOK

The opening lines of *Romeo and Juliet*, spoken by the Chorus, mention the 'pair of star-crossed lovers' who 'take their life' – from the beginning of the play, the fate of Romeo and Juliet is carved in stone, preordained by the heavens.

Finally, given that *Cold Mountain* crosses the ostensible boundaries of genre into romance and historical adventure, it is the scope of the modern novel that allows this freedom and Frazier has used the leeway to its fullest extent. Setting it during the American Civil War offers him scope to tackle a key phase in his own national history, and to make use of his own family folklore – evidence of the roomy potential of the novel genre.

HISTORICAL BACKGROUND
THE AMERICAN CIVIL WAR

South Carolina was one of the most prosperous Southern states in 1850s and 1860s America. Its wealth was largely built on the crops of indigo, rice and cotton. North Carolina was more mountainous, and in comparison a poorer state, with less industry and fewer trade links to the rest of the world.

On the national level, an unstable political situation had been brewing since the early part of the century. In 1861 this instability led to the outbreak of war at the garrison in Charleston, South Carolina. This incident took place against a wider backdrop of conflict among the various states which made up the Union. The principal issue at stake was self-governance, and more precisely whether or not slavery was to be allowed in new states as they applied to join the Union.

A balance of power had existed between Southern and Northern states until 1819, but during the 1830s and 1840s bitter campaigns took place: the North called for the unconditional emancipation of African American slaves, while the South was rigidly set against their emancipation.

Abraham Lincoln was elected to the presidency of the Union in 1860, running a campaign which aimed to wipe out slavery from all new territories wishing to join in future. As a result, South Carolina seceded from the Union in protest and in 1861 six more states joined the protest. The Federal garrison at Fort Sumter in Charleston was attacked by rebels (Confederates) in April 1861, and President Lincoln retaliated with a blockade of all Southern ports. It was clear that this would have huge economic and trade implications for the Southern states, and war broke out. In May North Carolina seceded along with three other Southern states.

The Confederacy asserted its right to run life along the lines it knew, and included slavery in this status quo. Abraham Lincoln was fiercely for the Union, and even asserted that if he could preserve it from dissolution by not freeing any slaves, he would. But by 1863 he proclaimed the emancipation of slaves in rebel states, though of

 CHECK THE NET

Information on the generals of both sides in the war can be found at **www. civilwarhome. com**; go to Civil War Biographies. This site also has many links to related topics of the war.

course the war carried on for another two years. By 1865, when the Confederates under General Robert E. Lee surrendered to General Ulysses S. Grant at Appomattox Court House in Virginia, the constitution of the Union prohibited slavery anywhere in the United States. North and South Carolina were among some of the last states to be taken by Federal forces.

INDIAN REMOVAL ACT

Another significant social question of the time was the Indian Removal Act of 1830. Under this law the Cherokee people were forcibly removed from their land and made to march along what came to be known as the Trail of Tears to reservations in Oklahoma. The terrible suffering of this time is felt in much of Frazier's novel, particularly through his depiction of the woman left behind after the Cherokee departure, and also through Ada's sense of desperate loss in the Cherokee village.

SOCIAL VALUES

It is interesting to consider the extent to which Frazier's characters reflect the values of the time in which the book is set. Monroe, we learn from Ada's memories, was a devotee of Ralph Waldo Emerson and existed in an abstract world of ideas and intellectual rigour, shown in his determination to preach high philosophical fragments to his congregation. Ada likewise tells Ruby stories from Greek myths. Socially, though, Ada's nature is to stand up for herself, and her 'proto-feminist' outlook – not wishing to marry or to play the marriage game – would have been remarkable for a woman of her class and upbringing.

Ruby, on the other hand, shows an ambivalence about wealth and education, the war, the Federals and the Confederates – indeed about most structures outside daily survival. For all its proximity to some of the bloodiest and most fiercely fought battles of the Civil War, the local communities of North Carolina would, evidence suggests, have been similarly ambivalent: all aggressors, it appears, would have brought instability and trouble. The Swangers' wish to see their sons back farming would have been typical of the wish for status quo to resume.

QUESTION

Emerson wrote in *American Civilization* in 1862: 'War organises and forces individuals to combine and act with larger views.' To what extent is *Cold Mountain* about the individual acting for himself?

NORTH CAROLINA AND RELEVANT GEOGRAPHY

The novel centres on and around Cold Mountain, which is in a region of the Smoky Mountains called the Shining Rock Wilderness and in Pisgah National Forest. Near by is the Blue Ridge, which Inman plans to escape over into Virginia to see out the war on the Federal side. For readers unfamiliar with the geography of the region, a sense of the landscape, the valleys, plains and higher ground will undoubtedly help place the action, especially so in a novel which is so much centred on journeys and crossing terrain.

The North Carolina and Virginia mountainous borderland is Inman's home; Ada has come to live there from South Carolina, which was the first state to secede from the Union. The Carolinas differed markedly in the nineteenth century in terms of their wealth and agricultural economy, including the use of slave labour; this was a staple of the South Carolina economy, based on indigo, rice and cotton. North Carolina was a more isolated region, with smaller farmsteads, the remnants of Cherokee culture still strongly felt (and their passing lamented), and indigenous ways of life less affected than in the relatively sophisticated town of Charleston. Monroe's decision to move and find a healthier life showed his independence of mind and by association his daughter's own spirited nature. Inman and Ada are both from Confederate states but are realistic enough to see that the future lies in accepting the Federal line, even if only to survive.

Inman travels over flat land from his hospital to the mountains and sees it as inhospitable and 'foul' (Chapter 3, p. 65). He is a man of the mountains; he has grazed livestock on the high balds, met with Cherokee boys and is fully conversant with the indigenous culture. Ada has a further set of reference points in her life: Western 'high' culture, philosophy, art, literature and a comfortable affluent lifestyle all epitomised by the town of Charleston.

CHECK THE BOOK

Inman's memory of the high balds on Balsam Mountain gives a precise geographical reference to an area of the Smoky Mountains. These, according to Bill Bryson's *A Walk in the Woods: Rediscovering America on the Appalachian Trail* (1998), are lavishly full of trees, flowers, fungi and mammals, owing to their topography and geological history. Bryson also describes the balds as grazing ground for livestock used by both Native Americans and European settlers.

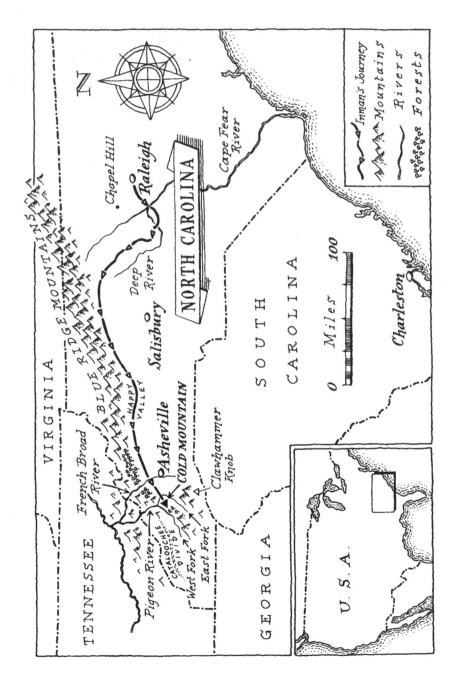

World events	Charles Frazier's life	Literary events
1776 July 4 American Declaration of Independence		
1789 French Revolution		
		1791 Publication of William Bartram's *Travels*
		1798 Publication of *Lyrical Ballads* by William Wordsworth and Samuel Taylor Coleridge, generally considered to be the birth of English Romanticism
		1818 John Keats, *Endymion*
		1819 Mary Ann Evans (George Eliot) born
1830 Indian Removal Act		
		1836 Ralph Waldo Emerson, *Nature*
1838–9 Trail of Tears		
		1850 Death of Wordsworth; Nathaniel Hawthorne, *The Scarlet Letter*
		1851 Herman Melville, *Moby Dick*
		1852 Harriet Beecher Stowe, *Uncle Tom's Cabin*
		1859 Charles Darwin, *On the Origin of Species by Means of Natural Selection*; George Eliot, *Adam Bede*
1860 Election of Abraham Lincoln to presidency of United States; secession of South Carolina from Union		**1860** George Eliot, *The Mill on the Floss*

World events	Charles Frazier's life	Literary events
1861 February Six other states secede; Confederate States of America formed; (April) first shots fired at Fort Sumter; American Civil War begins		
1863 Gettysburg Address		
1865 Confederates surrender at Appomattox; Abraham Lincoln assassinated		**1865–9** Leo Tolstoy, *War and Peace*
		1903 W. E. B. Du Bois, *The Souls of the Black Folk*
1917 United States enters First World War		
		1925 F. Scott Fitzgerald, *The Great Gatsby*
1929 Stock market crash		**1929** Ernest Hemingway, *A Farewell to Arms*; William Faulkner, *The Sound and the Fury*
		1930 William Faulkner, *As I Lay Dying*
1941 Pearl Harbour attacked; United States enters Second World War		
1945 Atomic bombs dropped on Hiroshima and Nagasaki; end of Second World War		
		1947 Tennessee Williams, *A Streetcar Named Desire*
		1949 Arthur Miller, *Death of a Salesman*
1950–4 McCarthy 'witch-hunts'	**1950** Born in Asheville, North Carolina	
		1953 Arthur Miller, *The Crucible*

World events	Charles Frazier's life	Literary events
1955 Rosa Parks arrested for refusing to give up her seat on a bus in Alabama		
1962 Cuban missile crisis		
1963 President John F. Kennedy assassinated		
1964 Civil Rights Act		
1968 Martin Luther King assassinated		
1965–73 Vietnam War		
		1970 Dee Brown, *Bury My Heart at Wounded Knee: An Indian History of the American West*
	1973 BA from University of North Carolina	
1974 President Richard Nixon resigns		
		1982 Alice Walker, *The Color Purple*
	1986 PhD from University of South Carolina	
		1987 Toni Morrison, *Beloved*
1990 Iraq invades Kuwait		
1991 First Gulf War begins		
	1997 *Cold Mountain* published and wins National Book Award and Notable Book of the Year Award	
	2003 Film of *Cold Mountain*, directed by Anthony Minghella	
		2005 E. L. Doctorow, *The March*

FURTHER READING

Peter Barry, *Beginning Theory: An Introduction to Literary and Cultural Theory*, Manchester University Press, 1995

Nina Baym, 'Melodramas of Beset Manhood: How Theories of American Fiction Exclude Women Authors', in Gordon Hutner, ed., *American Literature, American Culture*, Oxford University Press, 1998

Bill Bryson, *A Walk in the Woods*, Reed Business Edition, 1998

Lawrence Buell, 'American Literary Emergence as a Postcolonial Phenomenon', in Gordon Hutner, ed., *American Literature, American Culture*, Oxford University Press, 1998

Joseph Campbell, *The Hero with a Thousand Faces* (Bollingen Series), Princeton University Press, 1990 (first published 1949)

Marcus Cunliffe, *The Literature of the United States*, Penguin, 1986 (first published 1954)

E. L. Doctorow, *The March*, Random House, 2005

Margaret Drabble, ed., *The Oxford Companion to English Literature*, Oxford University Press, 2000 (sixth edition)

Kevin Grauke, 'Vietnam, Survivalism and the Civil War: The Use of History in Michael Shaara's *The Killer Angels* and Charles Frazier's *Cold Mountain*', in *War, Literature, and the Arts (WLA)*, 2002

Robert Herrick, 'The American Novel', in Gordon Hutner, ed., *American Literature, American Culture*, Oxford University Press, 1998

Alfred Kazin, *On Native Grounds: An Interpretation of Modern American Prose Literature*, Harvest Books, 1942

Barry Lopez, 'A Literature of Place', The EnviroLink Network, 1997, http://arts.envirolink.org

Michael McKeon, *Theory of the Novel: A Historical Approach*, Johns Hopkins University Press, 2000

John Peck, *How to Study a Novel*, Palgrave, 1995

Edward W. Said, *Culture and Imperialism*, Vintage, 1994

Simon Schama, *Landscape and Memory*, HarperCollins, 1995

allegory the representation of morals or ideas by specific figures, characters or events in a novel, play or poem, often extended into a narrative

alter ego another, possibly darker, side of one's self

analepsis see **flashback**

anti-hero a character who lacks the special qualities that make a hero, and functions somewhat as a contrast to the heroic qualities of a protagonist

apotheosis the elevation to a high rank or status, or a transcendental state, becoming godlike

archaisms words from antiquated or old-fashioned language, which have fallen out of common use

bathos an anticlimax or a sudden transition in literary style or events in a story

dissonance when ideas or moods lack harmony and show conflict

elegiac expressing sorrow for something that is lost

embedded narrative a piece of another story inserted into the main account

epic a form of literature which uses **mythical** figures or events to show truths about human nature; often set in times of war or civil conflict, and on a superhuman or godlike stage

flashback where the narrative takes the reader back to an earlier part of the story

foreshadow to give an indication of future events by a sign earlier on

hyperbole exaggeration in a literary text

irony when events work against the main thrust of a story, for example suddenly turning for or against the protagonist; or the use of language to indicate something beneath the surface truth

lyrical poetic, often lilting language which is characterised by beauty of sight, sound, or other sensuous qualities

motif a theme or idea which recurs in a text

myth a traditional story, often of a hero or powerful figure, sometimes involving the supernatural, or pitting gods against humans

naturalism a literary movement which works on the premise that human beings are subject to and ruled by outside forces, and have little self-determination; post-Darwinian in context

LITERARY TERMS

omniscient narrator a detached third-person narrator who appears to understand and know the characters on the inside, and observes them as they make decisions

persona the role or set of characteristics making up a character, often seen from one side more exclusively than another (for example Ada's early persona is of a well-educated and confident woman, though the fact is, and the narrative tells us, that she lacks self-assurance)

picaresque a type of narrative where the characters are comic, self-important and often ridiculous figures who operate in a corrupt society

portents omens which foretell the future

realist a description applied to literature, which aims to present reality as it is, and uses everyday characters, dialogue and situations to do so

syntax the word order, or grammar, which conveys meaning

tableau a scene in a novel or play in which events seem to have paused for the reader or audience to absorb a particular message

totemic something which belongs to a social group and operates as a special emblem of their values

Transcendentalism a nineteenth-century philosophical and social movement which believed divinity was present in all nature and humanity

vernacular the local or regional dialect of a people

vignette a short emblematic description or interaction between characters

Helen Treutler is a sixth-form college lecturer in English in East Sussex. She has taught adults, and now teaches all levels of the sixteen to nineteen age group. She has a particular interest in American literature, specifically drama and the late twentieth-century novel. She took her degree in English Literature at Cambridge University in 1987 and qualified as a teacher in 1997.

NOTES

Maya Angelou
I Know Why the Caged Bird Sings

Jane Austen
Pride and Prejudice

Alan Ayckbourn
Absent Friends

Elizabeth Barrett Browning
Selected Poems

Robert Bolt
A Man for All Seasons

Harold Brighouse
Hobson's Choice

Charlotte Brontë
Jane Eyre

Emily Brontë
Wuthering Heights

Brian Clark
Whose Life is it Anyway?

Robert Cormier
Heroes

Shelagh Delaney
A Taste of Honey

Charles Dickens
David Copperfield
Great Expectations
Hard Times
Oliver Twist
Selected Stories

Roddy Doyle
Paddy Clarke Ha Ha Ha

George Eliot
Silas Marner
The Mill on the Floss

Anne Frank
The Diary of a Young Girl

William Golding
Lord of the Flies

Oliver Goldsmith
She Stoops to Conquer

Willis Hall
The Long and the Short and the Tall

Thomas Hardy
Far from the Madding Crowd
The Mayor of Casterbridge
Tess of the d'Urbervilles
The Withered Arm and other Wessex Tales

L. P. Hartley
The Go-Between

Seamus Heaney
Selected Poems

Susan Hill
I'm the King of the Castle

Barry Hines
A Kestrel for a Knave

Louise Lawrence
Children of the Dust

Harper Lee
To Kill a Mockingbird

Laurie Lee
Cider with Rosie

Arthur Miller
The Crucible
A View from the Bridge

Robert O'Brien
Z for Zachariah

Frank O'Connor
My Oedipus Complex and Other Stories

George Orwell
Animal Farm

J. B. Priestley
An Inspector Calls
When We Are Married

Willy Russell
Educating Rita
Our Day Out

J. D. Salinger
The Catcher in the Rye

William Shakespeare
Henry IV Part I
Henry V
Julius Caesar
Macbeth
The Merchant of Venice
A Midsummer Night's Dream
Much Ado About Nothing
Romeo and Juliet
The Tempest
Twelfth Night

George Bernard Shaw
Pygmalion

Mary Shelley
Frankenstein

R. C. Sherriff
Journey's End

Rukshana Smith
Salt on the snow

John Steinbeck
Of Mice and Men

Robert Louis Stevenson
Dr Jekyll and Mr Hyde

Jonathan Swift
Gulliver's Travels

Robert Swindells
Daz 4 Zoe

Mildred D. Taylor
Roll of Thunder, Hear My Cry

Mark Twain
Huckleberry Finn

James Watson
Talking in Whispers

Edith Wharton
Ethan Frome

William Wordsworth
Selected Poems

A Choice of Poets

Mystery Stories of the Nineteenth Century including The Signalman

Nineteenth Century Short Stories

Poetry of the First World War

Six Women Poets

For the AQA Anthology:

Duffy and Armitage & Pre-1914 Poetry

Heaney and Clarke & Pre-1914 Poetry

Poems from Different Cultures

Margaret Atwood
Cat's Eye
The Handmaid's Tale
Jane Austen
Emma
Mansfield Park
Persuasion
Pride and Prejudice
Sense and Sensibility
William Blake
Songs of Innocence and of Experience
Charlotte Brontë
Jane Eyre
Villette
Emily Brontë
Wuthering Heights
Angela Carter
Nights at the Circus
Wise Children
Geoffrey Chaucer
The Franklin's Prologue and Tale
The Merchant's Prologue and Tale
The Miller's Prologue and Tale
The Prologue to the Canterbury Tales
The Wife of Bath's Prologue and Tale
Samuel Coleridge
Selected Poems
Joseph Conrad
Heart of Darkness
Daniel Defoe
Moll Flanders
Charles Dickens
Bleak House
Great Expectations
Hard Times
Emily Dickinson
Selected Poems
John Donne
Selected Poems
Carol Ann Duffy
Selected Poems
George Eliot
Middlemarch
The Mill on the Floss
T. S. Eliot
Selected Poems
The Waste Land
F. Scott Fitzgerald
The Great Gatsby

E. M. Forster
A Passage to India
Charles Frazier
Cold Mountain
Brian Friel
Making History
Translations
William Golding
The Spire
Thomas Hardy
Jude the Obscure
The Mayor of Casterbridge
The Return of the Native
Selected Poems
Tess of the d'Urbervilles
Seamus Heaney
Selected Poems from 'Opened Ground
Nathaniel Hawthorne
The Scarlet Letter
Homer
The Iliad
The Odyssey
Aldous Huxley
Brave New World
Kazuo Ishiguro
The Remains of the Day
Ben Jonson
The Alchemist
James Joyce
Dubliners
John Keats
Selected Poems
Philip Larkin
The Whitsun Weddings and Selected Poems
Ian McEwan
Atonement
Christopher Marlowe
Doctor Faustus
Edward II
Arthur Miller
Death of a Salesman
John Milton
Paradise Lost Books I & II
Toni Morrison
Beloved
George Orwell
Nineteen Eighty-Four
Sylvia Plath
Selected Poems
Alexander Pope
Rape of the Lock & Selected Poems

William Shakespeare
Antony and Cleopatra
As You Like It
Hamlet
Henry IV Part I
King Lear
Macbeth
Measure for Measure
The Merchant of Venice
A Midsummer Night's Dream
Much Ado About Nothing
Othello
Richard II
Richard III
Romeo and Juliet
The Taming of the Shrew
The Tempest
Twelfth Night
The Winter's Tale
George Bernard Shaw
Saint Joan
Mary Shelley
Frankenstein
Bram Stoker
Dracula
Jonathan Swift
Gulliver's Travels and A Modest Proposal
Alfred Tennyson
Selected Poems
Alice Walker
The Color Purple
Oscar Wilde
The Importance of Being Earnest
Tennessee Williams
A Streetcar Named Desire
The Glass Menagerie
Jeanette Winterson
Oranges Are Not the Only Fruit
John Webster
The Duchess of Malfi
Virginia Woolf
To the Lighthouse
William Wordsworth
The Prelude and Selected Poems
W. B. Yeats
Selected Poems
Metaphysical Poets